MznLnx

Missing Links Exam Preps

Exam Prep for

MP Financial Accounting: Information for Decisions

Wild, 4th Edition

The MznLnx Exam Prep is your link from the texbook and lecture to your exams.
The MznLnx Exam Preps are unauthorized and comprehensive reviews of your textbooks.

All material provided by MznLnx and Rico Publications (c) 2010
Textbook publishers and textbook authors do not particpate in or contribute to these reviews.

MznLnx

Rico
Publications

Exam Prep for MP Financial Accounting: Information for Decisions
4th Edition
Wild

Publisher: Raymond Houge
Assistant Editor: Michael Rouger
Text and Cover Designer: Lisa Buckner
Marketing Manager: Sara Swagger
Project Manager, Editorial Production: Jerry Emerson
Art Director: Vernon Lowerui

Product Manager: Dave Mason
Editorial Assitant: Rachel Guzmanji
Pedagogy: Debra Long
Cover Image: Jim Reed/Getty Images
Text and Cover Printer: City Printing, Inc.
Compositor: Media Mix, Inc.

(c) 2010 Rico Publications
ALL RIGHTS RESERVED. No part of this work covered by the copyright may be reproduced or used in any form or by an means--graphic, electronic, or mechanical, including photocopying, recording, taping, Web distribution, information storage, and retrieval systems, or in any other manner--without the written permission of the publisher.

Printed in the United States
ISBN:

For more information about our products, contact us at:
Dave.Mason@RicoPublications.com

For permission to use material from this text or product, submit a request online to:
Dave.Mason@RicoPublications.com

Contents

CHAPTER 1
Introducing Accounting in Business — 1

CHAPTER 2
Analyzing and Recording Transactions — 17

CHAPTER 3
Adjusting Accounts and Preparing Financial Statements — 28

CHAPTER 4
Reporting and Analyzing Merchandising Operations — 40

CHAPTER 5
Reporting and Analyzing Inventories — 48

CHAPTER 6
Reporting and Analyzing Cash and Internal Controls — 54

CHAPTER 7
Reporting and Analyzing Receivables — 69

CHAPTER 8
Reporting and Analyzing Long-Term Assets — 77

CHAPTER 9
Reporting and Analyzing Current Liabilities — 89

CHAPTER 10
Reporting and Analyzing Long-Term Liabilities — 101

CHAPTER 11
Reporting and Analyzing Equity — 112

CHAPTER 12
Reporting and Analyzing Cash Flows — 125

CHAPTER 13
Analyzing and Interpreting Financial Statements — 136

ANSWER KEY — 150

TO THE STUDENT

COMPREHENSIVE

The *MznLnx* Exam Prep series is designed to help you pass your exams. Editors at MznLnx review your textbooks and then prepare these practice exams to help you master the textbook material. Unlike study guides, workbooks, and practice tests provided by the texbook publisher and textbook authors, *MznLnx* gives you **all** of the material in each chapter in exam form, not just samples, so you can be sure to nail your exam.

MECHANICAL

The MznLnx Exam Prep series creates exams that will help you learn the subject matter as well as test you on your understanding. Each question is designed to help you master the concept. Just working through the exams, you gain an understanding of the subject--its a simple mechanical process that produces success.

INTEGRATED STUDY GUIDE AND REVIEW

MznLnx is not just a set of exams designed to test you, its also a comprehensive review of the subject content. Each exam question is also a review of the concept, making sure that you will get the answer correct without having to go to other sources of material. You learn as you go! Its the easiest way to pass an exam.

HUMOR

Studying can be tedious and dry. MznLnx's instructional design includes moderate humor within the exam questions on occassion, to break the tedium and revitalize the brain

Chapter 1. Introducing Accounting in Business   1

1. A _____ is a body of elected or appointed members who jointly oversee the activities of a company or organization. The body sometimes has a different name, such as board of trustees, board of governors, board of managers, or executive board. It is often simply referred to as 'the board.'

A board's activities are determined by the powers, duties, and responsibilities delegated to it or conferred on it by an authority outside itself.

   a. Hospital Survey and Construction Act
   b. Chief Financial Officers Act of 1990
   c. Consumer protection laws
   d. Board of directors

2. _____ is the recording of the value of assets, liabilities, income, and expenses in the daybooks, journals, and ledgers, in which debit and credit entries are chronologically posted to record changes in value. _____ is often mistaken for accounting, which is the system of recording, verifying, and reporting such information. Practitioners of accounting are called accountants.
   a. Bookkeeping
   b. Double-entry bookkeeping
   c. Debit and credit
   d. Controlling account

3. Employment is a contract between two parties, one being the employer and the other being the _____. An _____ may be defined as: 'A person in the service of another under any contract of hire, express or implied, oral or written, where the employer has the power or right to control and direct the _____ in the material details of how the work is to be performed.' Black's Law Dictionary page 471 (5th ed. 1979.)
   a. AMEX
   b. ABC Television Network
   c. Employee
   d. AIG

4. An _____ is an audit professional who performs an audit on the financial statements of a company, government, individual and who is independent of the entity being audited. Users of these entities' financial information, such as investors, government agencies, and the general public, rely on the _____ to present an unbiased and independent evaluation on such entities. They are distinguished from internal auditors for two main reasons: (1) the internal auditor's primary responsibility is appraising an entity's risk management strategy and practices, management (including IT) control frameworks and governance processes, and (2) they do not express an opinion on the entity's financial statements.
   a. Event data
   b. International Federation of Audit Bureaux of Circulations
   c. Audit risk
   d. External auditor

5. An _____ is a term used in behavioral economics to describe those types of behaviors that impose costs on a person in the long-run that are not taken into account when making decisions in the present. Classical Economics discourages government from creating legislation that targets internalities, because it is assumed that the consumer takes these personal costs into account when paying for the good that causes the _____. For example, cigarettes should be taxed because of the negative consumption externalities that they impose, such as second-hand smoke, not because the smoker harms him or herself by smoking.
   a. Operating budget
   b. Inventory turnover ratio
   c. Internality
   d. Authorised capital

Chapter 1. Introducing Accounting in Business

6. The _____ is the United States federal government agency that collects taxes and enforces the internal revenue laws. It is an agency within the U.S. Dept of the treasury responsible for interpretation and application of Federal tax law. The official U.S. Treasury regulations provide (in part):

The _____ is a bureau of the Department of the Treasury under the immediate direction of the Commissioner of Internal Revenue.

   a. Indirect tax   b. Use tax
   c. Internal Revenue Service   d. Income tax

7. A loan is a type of debt. Like all debt instruments, a loan entails the redistribution of financial assets over time, between the _____ and the borrower.

In a loan, the borrower initially receives or borrows an amount of money, called the principal, from the _____, and is obligated to pay back or repay an equal amount of money to the _____ at a later time.

   a. Loan to value   b. Debt
   c. Credit rating   d. Lender

8. A mutual shareholder or _____ is an individual or company (including a corporation) that legally owns one or more shares of stock in a joint stock company. A company's shareholders collectively own that company. Thus, the typical goal of such companies is to enhance shareholder value.

   a. Growth investing   b. 3M Company
   c. Stock split   d. Stockholder

9. The general definition of an _____ is an evaluation of a person, organization, system, process, project or product. _____s are performed to ascertain the validity and reliability of information; also to provide an assessment of a system's internal control. The goal of an _____ is to express an opinion on the person/organization/system (etc) in question, under evaluation based on work done on a test basis.

   a. Audit regime   b. Institute of Chartered Accountants of India
   c. Assurance service   d. Audit

10. _____ are formal records of a business' financial activities.

In British English, including United Kingdom company law, _____ are often referred to as accounts, although the term _____ is also used, particularly by accountants.

_____ provide an overview of a business' financial condition in both short and long term.

   a. 3M Company   b. Financial statements
   c. Notes to the financial statements   d. Statement of retained earnings

Chapter 1. Introducing Accounting in Business

11. _____ is the statutory title of qualified accountants in the United States who have passed the Uniform _____ Examination and have met additional state education and experience requirements for certification as a _____. Individuals who have passed the Exam but have not either accomplished the required on-the-job experience or have previously met it but in the meantime have lapsed their continuing professional education are, in many states, permitted the designation '_____ Inactive' or an equivalent phrase. In most U.S. states, only _____s who are licensed are able to provide to the public attestation (including auditing) opinions on financial statements.
   - a. Certified public accountant
   - b. Chartered Certified Accountant
   - c. Chartered Accountant
   - d. Certified General Accountant

12. A _____, also client, buyer or purchaser is the buyer or user of the paid products of an individual or organization, mostly called the supplier or seller. This is typically through purchasing or renting goods or services.
   - a. BNSF Railway
   - b. BMC Software, Inc.
   - c. Customer
   - d. 3M Company

13. The _____ is a private, not-for-profit organization whose primary purpose is to develop generally accepted accounting principles (GAAP) within the United States in the public's interest. The Securities and Exchange Commission (SEC) designated the _____ as the organization responsible for setting accounting standards for public companies in the U.S. It was created in 1973, replacing the Accounting Principles Board and the Committee on Accounting Procedure of the American Institute of Certified Public Accountants. The _____'s mission is 'to establish and improve standards of financial accounting and reporting for the guidance and education of the public, including issuers, auditors, and users of financial information.'

The _____ is not a governmental body.

   - a. Financial Accounting Standards Board
   - b. Fannie Mae
   - c. Governmental Accounting Standards Board
   - d. Public company

14. In accounting and organizational theory, _____ is defined as a process effected by an organization's structure, work and authority flows, people and management information systems, designed to help the organization accomplish specific goals or objectives. It is a means by which an organization's resources are directed, monitored, and measured. It plays an important role in preventing and detecting fraud and protecting the organization's resources, both physical (e.g., machinery and property) and intangible (e.g., reputation or intellectual property such as trademarks.)
   - a. Internal control
   - b. Auditor independence
   - c. Audit committee
   - d. Audit risk

15. _____ is concerned with the provisions and use of accounting information to managers within organizations, to provide them with the basis to make informed business decisions that will allow them to be better equipped in their management and control functions.

In contrast to financial accountancy information, _____ information is:

   - usually confidential and used by management, instead of publicly reported;
   - forward-looking, instead of historical;
   - pragmatically computed using extensive management information systems and internal controls, instead of complying with accounting standards.

This is because of the different emphasis: _____ information is used within an organization, typically for decision-making.

   a. Governmental accounting
   c. Grenzplankostenrechnung
   b. Nonassurance services
   d. Management accounting

16. A _____ is a computer application that simulates a paper worksheet. It displays multiple cells that together make up a grid consisting of rows and columns, each cell containing either alphanumeric text or numeric values. A _____ cell may alternatively contain a formula that defines how the contents of that cell is to be calculated from the contents of any other cell (or combination of cells) each time any cell is updated.

   a. Mutual fund
   c. Merck ' Co., Inc.
   b. Linear regression
   d. Spreadsheet

17. An _____ is a practitioner of accountancy, which is the measurement, disclosure or provision of assurance about financial information that helps managers, investors, tax authorities and other decision makers make resource allocation decisions.

The word '_____' is derived from the French 'Compter' which took its origin from the Latin 'Computare'. The word was formerly written in English as 'Accomptant', but in process of time the word, which was always pronounced by dropping the 'p', became gradually changed both in pronunciation and in orthography to its present form.

   a. AMEX
   c. AIG
   b. ABC Television Network
   d. Accountant

18. The _____ designation is an exam-based payroll certification attained by individuals who possess a high level of professional competency through both the acquisition of knowledge and direct payroll experience.

Prior to sitting for the exam, a _____ candidate must verify employment in the payroll profession preceding the exam date. The _____ designation indicates that an individual has the experience and skills necessary to provide strategic payroll management and support to facilitate a companye;s overall business goals.

   a. 3M Company
   c. BMC Software, Inc.
   b. BNSF Railway
   d. Certified payroll professional

19. The _____ of a company or public agency is the corporate officer primarily responsible for managing the financial risks of the business or agency. This officer is also responsible for financial planning and record-keeping, as well as financial reporting to higher management. (In recent years, however, the role has expanded to encompass communicating financial performance and forecasts to the analyst community.)

   a. Merck ' Co., Inc.
   c. Chief financial officer
   b. Chief executive officer
   d. NASDAQ

20. Bookkeeping is the recording of financial transactions. Transactions include sales, purchases, income, and payments by an individual or organization. Bookkeeping is usually performed by a _____.

Chapter 1. Introducing Accounting in Business

a. Double-entry bookkeeping
b. Bookkeeping
c. Bookkeeper
d. Debit and credit

21. Internal auditing is a profession and activity involved in helping organisations achieve their stated objectives. It does this by utilizing a systematic methodology for analyzing business processes, procedures and activities with the goal of highlighting organizational problems and recommending solutions. Professionals called _____ are employed by organizations to perform the internal auditing activity.

a. Auditing Standards Board
b. Auditor independence
c. Internal Auditing
d. Internal auditors

22. In a company, _____ is the sum of all financial records of salaries, wages, bonuses and deductions.

A paycheck, is traditionally a paper document issued by an employer to pay an employee for services rendered. While most commonly used in the United States, recently the physical paycheck has been increasingly replaced by electronic direct deposit to bank accounts.

a. 3M Company
b. Tax expense
c. Total Expense Ratio
d. Payroll

23. The _____ is the national, professional association of CPAs in the United States, with more than 330,000 members, including CPAs in business and industry, public practice, government, and education; student affiliates; and international associates. It sets ethical standards for the profession and U.S. auditing standards for audits of private companies; federal, state and local governments; and non-profit organizations.

Approximately 40% of its members are engaged in the practice of public accounting, in areas such as auditing, accounting, taxation, general business consulting, business valuation, personal financial planning and business technology.

a. Other postemployment benefits
b. ABC Television Network
c. American Institute of Certified Public Accountants
d. AIG

24. In mathematics, two elements x and y of a set partially ordered by a relation ≤ are said to be _____ if and only if x ≤ y or y ≤ x if and only if x < y or y < x or y = x. For example, two sets are _____ with respect to inclusion if and only if one is a subset of the other.

In a classification of mathematical objects such as topological spaces, two criteria are said to be _____ when the objects that obey one criterion constitute a subset of the objects that obey the other one .

a. Scientific Research and Experimental Development Tax Incentive Program
b. Database auditing
c. Comparable
d. Consumption

25. _____ is the term used to refer to the standard framework of guidelines for financial accounting used in any given jurisdiction. _____ includes the standards, conventions, and rules accountants follow in recording and summarizing transactions, and in the preparation of financial statements.

6   Chapter 1. Introducing Accounting in Business

Financial accounting information must be assembled and reported objectively.

a. General ledger
b. Current asset
c. Long-term liabilities
d. Generally accepted accounting principles

26. _____ represents claims for which formal instruments of credit are issued as evidence of debt, such as a promissory note. The credit instrument normally requires the debtor to pay interest and extends for time periods of 60-90 days or longer.
a. Public offering
b. Notes receivable
c. Moving average
d. Restricted stock

27. The _____ of 2002 (Pub.L. 107-204, 116 Stat. 745, enacted July 30, 2002), also known as the Public Company Accounting Reform and Investor Protection Act of 2002, is a United States federal law enacted on July 30, 2002 in response to a number of major corporate and accounting scandals including those affecting Enron, Tyco International, Adelphia, Peregrine Systems and WorldCom. The legislation establishes new or enhanced standards for all U.S. public company boards, management, and public accounting firms. It does not apply to privately held companies.
a. FCPA
b. Fair Labor Standards Act
c. Lease
d. Sarbanes-Oxley Act

28. In economics, business, retail, and accounting, a _____ is the value of money that has been used up to produce something, and hence is not available for use anymore. In economics, a _____ is an alternative that is given up as a result of a decision. In business, the _____ may be one of acquisition, in which case the amount of money expended to acquire it is counted as _____.
a. Prime cost
b. Cost of quality
c. Cost allocation
d. Cost

29. _____ was a maxim coined by Josiah Warren, indicating a (prescriptive) version of the labor theory of value. Warren maintained that the just compensation for labor (or for its product) could only be an equivalent amount of labor (or a product embodying an equivalent amount.) Thus, profit, rent, and interest were considered unjust economic arrangements.
a. Politicized issue
b. BMC Software, Inc.
c. 3M Company
d. Cost the limit of price

30. In accounting, _____ is the original monetary value of an economic item. In some circumstances, assets and liabilities may be shown at their _____, as if there had been no change in value since the date of acquisition. The balance sheet value of the item may therefore differ from the 'true' value.
a. Matching principle
b. Historical cost
c. Bottom line
d. Cost of goods sold

31. _____ are standards and interpretations adopted by the International Accounting Standards Board (IASB.)

Many of the standards forming part of _____ are known by the older name of International Accounting Standards (IAS.) IAS were issued between 1973 and 2001 by the board of the International Accounting Standards Committee (IASC.)

Chapter 1. Introducing Accounting in Business 7

   a. Out-of-pocket
   c. AIG
   b. ABC Television Network
   d. International Financial Reporting Standards

32. The _____ founded on April 1, 2001 is the successor of the International Accounting Standards Committee (IASC) founded in June 1973 in London. It is responsible for developing the International Financial Reporting Standards (new name for the International Accounting Standards issued after 2001), and promoting the use and application of these standards.

The _____ is an independent, privately-funded accounting standard-setter based in London, UK.

   a. Institute of Management Accountants
   c. Emerging technologies
   b. International Accounting Standards Board
   d. Information Systems Audit and Control Association

33. _____ is a concept whereby a person's financial liability is limited to a fixed sum, most commonly the value of a person's investment in a company or partnership with _____. A shareholder in a limited company is not personally liable for any of the debts of the company, other than for the value of his investment in that company. The same is true for the members of a _____ partnership and the limited partners in a limited partnership.
   a. Joint venture
   c. Due diligence
   b. Limited liability
   d. Burden of proof

34. A _____ is a partnership in which some or all partners (depending on the jurisdiction) have limited liability. It therefore exhibits elements of partnerships and corporations. In an _____ one partner is not responsible or liable for another partner's misconduct or negligence.
   a. Financial Accounting Standards Board
   c. Dow Jones ' Company
   b. Privately held
   d. Limited liability partnership

35. A _____ is a form of partnership similar to a general partnership, except that in addition to one or more general partners (GPs), there are one or more limited partners (_____s.) It is a partnership in which only one partner is required to be a general partner.

The GPs are, in all major respects, in the same legal position as partners in a conventional firm, i.e. they have management control, share the right to use partnership property, share the profits of the firm in predefined proportions, and have joint and several liability for the debts of the partnership.

   a. Minority interest
   c. Debenture
   b. Dow Jones ' Company
   d. Limited partnership

36. A _____ is a type of business entity in which partners (owners) share with each other the profits or losses of the business undertaking in which all have invested. _____s are often favored over corporations for taxation purposes, as the _____ structure does not generally incur a tax on profits before it is distributed to the partners (i.e. there is no dividend tax levied.) However, depending on the _____ structure and the jurisdiction in which it operates, owners of a _____ may be exposed to greater personal liability than they would as shareholders of a corporation.
   a. National Information Infrastructure Protection Act
   c. Partnership
   b. Resource Conservation and Recovery Act
   d. Corporate governance

37. _____ is any physical or virtual entity that is owned by an individual or jointly by a group of individuals. An owner of _____ has the right to consume, sell, rent, mortgage, transfer and exchange his or her _____. Important widely-recognized types of _____ include real _____, personal _____ (other physical possessions), and intellectual _____ (rights over artistic creations, inventions, etc.), although the latter is not always as widely recognized or enforced.

a. Fiduciary
b. Disclosure requirement
c. Primary authority
d. Property

38. _____, also known as property, plant, and equipment (PP&E), is a term used in accountancy for assets and property which cannot easily be converted into cash. This can be compared with current assets such as cash or bank accounts, which are described as liquid assets. In most cases, only tangible assets are referred to as fixed.

a. Bankruptcy prediction
b. Subledger
c. Minority interest
d. Fixed asset

39. _____ principle is a cornerstone of accrual accounting together with matching principle. They both determine the accounting period, in which revenues and expenses are recognized. According to the principle, revenues are recognized when they are (1) realized or realizable, and are (2) earned (usually when goods are transferred or services rendered), no matter when cash is received.

a. Revenue recognition
b. Net realizable value
c. BMC Software, Inc.
d. 3M Company

40. A _____ is the pinnacle activity involved in selling products or services in return for money or other compensation. It is an act of completion of a commercial activity.

A _____ is completed by the seller, the owner of the goods.

a. Tertiary sector of economy
b. Maturity
c. High yield stock
d. Sale

41. _____ is a fee paid on borrowed assets. It is the price paid for the use of borrowed money, or, money earned by deposited funds. Assets that are sometimes lent with _____ include money, shares, consumer goods through hire purchase, major assets such as aircraft, and even entire factories in finance lease arrangements. The _____ is calculated upon the value of the assets in the same manner as upon money.

a. AIG
b. ABC Television Network
c. Insolvency
d. Interest

42. In financial accounting, a _____ is defined as an obligation of an entity arising from past transactions or events, the settlement of which may result in the transfer or use of assets, provision of services or other yielding of economic benefits in the future.

a. False Claims Act
b. Corporate governance
c. Vested
d. Liability

43. A sole _____, or simply _____ is a type of business entity which legally has no separate existence from its owner. Hence, the limitations of liability enjoyed by a corporation and limited liability partnerships do not apply to sole proprietors. All debts of the business are debts of the owner.

Chapter 1. Introducing Accounting in Business

a. Pre-determined overhead rate
b. Proprietorship
c. Safety stock
d. Free cash flow

44. A _____, or simply proprietorship is a type of business entity which legally has no separate existence from its owner. Hence, the limitations of liability enjoyed by a corporation and limited liability partnerships do not apply to sole proprietors. All debts of the business are debts of the owner.

a. Customer satisfaction
b. Sole proprietorship
c. Time to market
d. Free cash flow

45. _____ is a form of corporation equity ownership represented in the securities. It is a stock whose dividends are based on market fluctuations. It is dangerous in comparison to preferred shares and some other investment options, in that in the event of bankruptcy, _____ investors receive their funds after preferred stock holders, bondholders, creditors, etc. On the other hand, common shares on average perform better than preferred shares or bonds over time.

a. Common stock
b. 3M Company
c. Stock split
d. Growth investing

46. _____ is the imposition of two or more taxes on the same income (in the case of income taxes), asset (in the case of capital taxes), or financial transaction (in the case of sales taxes.) It refers to two distinct situations:

- taxation of dividend income without relief or credit for taxes paid by the company paying the dividend on the income from which the dividend is paid. This arises in the so-called 'classical' system of corporate taxation, used in the United States.
- taxation by two or more countries of the same income, asset or transaction, for example income paid by an entity of one country to a resident of a different country. The double liability is often mitigated by tax treaties between countries.

It is not unusual for a business or individual who is resident in one country to make a taxable gain (earnings, profits) in another. This person may find that he is obliged by domestic laws to pay tax on that gain locally and pay again in the country in which the gain was made. Since this is inequitable, many nations make bilateral _____ agreements with each other.

a. Double taxation
b. Tax shelter
c. Federal Unemployment Tax Act
d. Carbon tax

47. The Federal National Mortgage Association (FNMA) (NYSE: FNM), commonly known as _____, is a stockholder-owned corporation chartered by Congress in 1968 as a government sponsored enterprise (GSE), but founded in 1938 during the Great Depression. The corporation's purpose is to purchase and securitize mortgages in order to ensure that funds are consistently available to the institutions that lend money to home buyers.

On September 7, 2008, James Lockhart, director of the Federal Housing Finance Agency (FHFA), announced that _____ and Freddie Mac were being placed into conservatorship of the FHFA.

a. Freddie Mac
b. Public company
c. National Conference of Commissioners on Uniform State Laws
d. Fannie Mae

Chapter 1. Introducing Accounting in Business

48. A _____ in the law of the vast majority of United States jurisdictions is a legal form of business company that provides limited liability to its owners. Often incorrectly called a 'limited liability corporation' (instead of company), it is a hybrid business entity having certain characteristics of both a corporation and a partnership. The primary characteristic an _____ shares with a corporation is limited liability, and the primary characteristic it shares with a partnership is the availability of pass-through income taxation.
    a. Bond market
    b. Data protection
    c. Consumer protection laws
    d. Limited liability company

49. The _____ is a United States federal law that imposes a federal employer tax used to fund state workforce agencies. Employers report this tax by filing an annual Form 940 with the Internal Revenue Service.
    a. Transfer tax
    b. Council Tax
    c. Federal Unemployment Tax Act
    d. Tax evasion

50. The basic _____ is the foundation for the double-entry bookkeeping system. It shows how assets were financed: either by borrowing money from someone (liability) or by paying your own money (shareholders' equity.)

    Assets = Liabilities + (Shareholders or Owners equity)

For example: A student buys a computer for $945.

    a. AIG
    b. Accounting equation
    c. AMEX
    d. ABC Television Network

51. _____ is a file or account that contains money that a person or company owes to suppliers, but has not paid yet (a form of debt.) When you receive an invoice you add it to the file, and then you remove it when you pay. Thus, the A/P is a form of credit that suppliers offer to their purchasers by allowing them to pay for a product or service after it has already been received.
    a. Earnings before interest, taxes, depreciation and amortization
    b. Accrual
    c. Accounts receivable
    d. Accounts payable

52. In business and accounting, _____ are everything of value that is owned by a person or company. It is a claim on the property your income of a borrower. The balance sheet of a firm records the monetary value of the _____ owned by the firm.
    a. Accounts receivable
    b. Assets
    c. Earnings before interest, taxes, depreciation and amortization
    d. Accrual basis accounting

53. _____ are payments made by a corporation to its shareholder members. It is the portion of corporate profits paid out to stockholders. When a corporation earns a profit or surplus, that money can be put to two uses: it can either be re-invested in the business (called retained earnings), or it can be paid to the shareholders as a dividend.
    a. Dividend stripping
    b. Dividend yield
    c. Dividend payout ratio
    d. Dividends

Chapter 1. Introducing Accounting in Business   11

54. _____, the Electronic Data-Gathering, Analysis, and Retrieval system, performs automated collection, validation, indexing, acceptance, and forwarding of submissions by companies and others who are required by law to file forms with the U.S. Securities and Exchange Commission (the 'SEC'.) The database is freely available to the public via Web or FTP, typically posting in excess of 3,000 filings per day.

Not all SEC filings by public companies are available on _____.

a. EDGAR
b. AIG
c. AMEX
d. ABC Television Network

55. In accounting, _____ has a very specific meaning. It is an outflow of cash or other valuable assets from a person or company to another person or company. This outflow of cash is generally one side of a trade for products or services that have equal or better current or future value to the buyer than to the seller.

a. ABC Television Network
b. AIG
c. Expense
d. AMEX

56. _____ is equal to the income that a firm has after subtracting costs and expenses from the total revenue. _____ can be distributed among holders of common stock as a dividend or held by the firm as retained earnings.

The items deducted will typically include tax expense, financing expense (interest expense), and minority interest. Likewise, preferred stock dividends will be subtracted too, though they are not an expense.

a. Matching principle
b. Long-term liabilities
c. Generally accepted accounting principles
d. Net income

57. _____ refers to a business or organization attempting to acquire goods or services to accomplish the goals of the enterprise. Though there are several organizations that attempt to set standards in the _____ process, processes can vary greatly between organizations. Typically the word e;_____e; is not used interchangeably with the word e;procuremente;, since procurement typically includes Expediting, Supplier Quality, and Traffic and Logistics (T'L) in addition to _____.

a. Free port
b. Purchasing
c. Consignor
d. Supply chain

58. A _____ is a fungible, negotiable instrument representing financial value. they are broadly categorized into debt securities (such as banknotes, bonds and debentures), and equity securities; e.g., common stocks. The company or other entity issuing the _____ is called the issuer.

a. BMC Software, Inc.
b. Security
c. Tracking stock
d. 3M Company

59. The U.S. _____ is an independent agency of the United States government which holds primary responsibility for enforcing the federal securities laws and regulating the securities industry, the nation's stock and options exchanges, and other electronic securities markets. The SEC was created by section 4 of the Securities Exchange Act of 1934 (now codified as 15 U.S.C. ÂÂ§ 78d and commonly referred to as the 1934 Act.)

a. Securities and Exchange Commission
b. 3M Company
c. BNSF Railway
d. BMC Software, Inc.

60. In economics, _____ or _____ goods or real _____ refers to factors of production used to create goods or services that are not themselves significantly consumed (though they may depreciate) in the production process. _____ goods may be acquired with money or financial _____. In finance and accounting, _____ generally refers to financial wealth, especially that used to start or maintain a business.

   a. Vyborg Appeal
   b. Capital
   c. Screening
   d. Disclosure

61. _____ is a specific term used in companies' financial reporting from the company-whole point of view. Because that use excludes the effects of changing ownership interest, an economic measure of _____ is necessary for financial analysis from the shareholders' point of view

_____ is defined by the Financial Accounting Standards Board, or FASB, as 'the change in equity [net assets] of a business enterprise during a period from transactions and other events and circumstances from nonowner sources. It includes all changes in equity during a period except those resulting from investments by owners and distributions to owners.'

_____ is the sum of net income and other items that must bypass the income statement because they have not been realized, including items like an unrealized holding gain or loss from available for sale securities and foreign currency translation gains or losses.

   a. Comprehensive income
   b. 3M Company
   c. BNSF Railway
   d. BMC Software, Inc.

62. A _____ is the transfer of wealth from one party (such as a person or company) to another. A _____ is usually made in exchange for the provision of goods, services or both, or to fulfill a legal obligation.

The simplest and oldest form of _____ is barter, the exchange of one good or service for another.

   a. 3M Company
   b. Payee
   c. BMC Software, Inc.
   d. Payment

63. _____ is one of a series of accounting transactions dealing with the billing of customers who owe money to a person, company or organization for goods and services that have been provided to the customer. In most business entities this is typically done by generating an invoice and mailing or electronically delivering it to the customer, who in turn must pay it within an established timeframe called credit or payment terms.

An example of a common payment term is Net 30, meaning payment is due in the amount of the invoice 30 days from the date of invoice.

   a. Adjusting entries
   b. Accrued revenue
   c. Accounts receivable
   d. Accrual

64. _____ is a company's financial statement that indicates how the revenue is transformed into the net income The purpose of the _____ is to show managers and investors whether the company made or lost money during the period being reported.

Chapter 1. Introducing Accounting in Business　　13

The important thing to remember about an _____ is that it represents a period of time.

a. AIG
b. ABC Television Network
c. AMEX
d. Income statement

65. In financial accounting, a _____ or statement of financial position is a summary of a person's or organization's balances. Assets, liabilities and ownership equity are listed as of a specific date, such as the end of its financial year. A _____ is often described as a snapshot of a company's financial condition.

a. Balance sheet
b. Financial statements
c. Statement of retained earnings
d. 3M Company

66. _____ is the balance of the amounts of cash being received and paid by a business during a defined period of time, sometimes tied to a specific project. Measurement of _____ can be used

- to evaluate the state or performance of a business or project.
- to determine problems with liquidity. Being profitable does not necessarily mean being liquid. A company can fail because of a shortage of cash, even while profitable.
- to project rate of returns. The time of _____s into and out of projects are used as inputs to financial models such as internal rate of return, and net present value.
- to examine income or growth of a business when it is believed that accrual accounting concepts do not represent economic realities. Alternately, _____ can be used to 'validate' the net income generated by accrual accounting.

_____ as a generic term may be used differently depending on context, and certain _____ definitions may be adapted by analysts and users for their own uses. Common terms include operating _____ and free _____.

a. Commercial paper
b. Cash flow
c. Flow-through entity
d. Controlling interest

67. In financial accounting, _____ , cash flow provided by operations or cash flow from operating activities, refers to the amount of cash a company generates from the revenues it brings in, excluding costs associated with long-term investment on capital items or investment in securities.

_____ = Cash generated from operations less taxation and interest paid, investment income received and less dividends paid gives rise to _____s per International Financial Reporting Standards.

To calculate cash generated from operations, one must calculate cash generated from customers and cash paid to suppliers.

a. AMEX
b. ABC Television Network
c. Operating cash flow
d. AIG

Chapter 1. Introducing Accounting in Business

68. In financial accounting, a _____ or Statement of cash flows is a financial statement that shows a company's flow of cash. The money coming into the business is called cash inflow, and money going out from the business is called cash outflow. The statement shows how changes in balance sheet and income accounts affect cash and cash equivalents, and breaks the analysis down to operating, investing, and financing activities.

   a. BNSF Railway
   b. BMC Software, Inc.
   c. 3M Company
   d. Cash flow statement

69. In economic models, the _____ time frame assumes no fixed factors of production. Firms can enter or leave the marketplace, and the cost (and availability) of land, labor, raw materials, and capital goods can be assumed to vary. In contrast, in the short-run time frame, certain factors are assumed to be fixed, because there is not sufficient time for them to change.

   a. Long-run
   b. Short-run
   c. BMC Software, Inc.
   d. 3M Company

70. _____ is a business, economics or investment term that refers to an asset's ability to be easily converted through an act of buying or selling without causing a significant movement in the price and with minimum loss of value. Money, or cash on hand, is the most liquid asset. An act of exchange of a less liquid asset with a more liquid asset is called liquidation.

   a. Transfer agent
   b. Financial instruments
   c. Spot rate
   d. Market liquidity

71. A _____ is any one of a variety of different systems, institutions, procedures, social relations and infrastructures whereby persons trade, and goods and services are exchanged, forming part of the economy. It is an arrangement that allows buyers and sellers to exchange things. _____s vary in size, range, geographic scale, location, types and variety of human communities, as well as the types of goods and services traded.

   a. Recession
   b. Market
   c. Perfect competition
   d. Market Failure

72. The _____ percentage shows how profitable a company's assets are in generating revenue.

   _____ can be computed as:

   $$ROA = \frac{\text{Net Income - Interest Expense - Interest Tax savings}}{\text{Average Total Assets}}$$

   This number tells you what the company can do with what it has, i.e. how many dollars of earnings they derive from each dollar of assets they control. Its a useful number for comparing competing companies in the same industry.

   a. Return on sales
   b. Statutory Liquidity Ratio
   c. Capital employed
   d. Return on assets

73. In finance, _____ also known as return on investment, rate of profit or sometimes just return, is the ratio of money gained or lost on an investment relative to the amount of money invested. The amount of money gained or lost may be referred to as interest, profit/loss, gain/loss, or net income/loss. The money invested may be referred to as the asset, capital, principal, or the cost basis of the investment.

a. Capital employed
b. Debt to capital ratio
c. Theoretical ex-rights price
d. Rate of return

74. In finance, or business _____ is the ability of an entity to pay its debts with available cash. _____ can also be described as the ability of a corporation to meet its long-term fixed expenses and to accomplish long-term expansion and growth. The better a company's _____, the better it is financially.
   a. 3M Company
   b. BMC Software, Inc.
   c. Capital asset
   d. Solvency

75. The _____, a ratio that is typically applied to banks, in simple terms is defined as expenses as a percentage of revenue (expenses / revenue), with a few variations. A lower percentage is better since that means expenses are low and earnings are high. It is related to operating leverage, which measures the ratio between fixed costs and variable costs.
   a. Operating leverage
   b. Equity ratio
   c. Average rate of return
   d. Efficiency ratio

76. _____ is a concept that denotes the precise probability of specific eventualities. Technically, the notion of _____ is independent from the notion of value and, as such, eventualities may have both beneficial and adverse consequences. However, in general usage the convention is to focus only on potential negative impact to some characteristic of value that may arise from a future event.
   a. Risk adjusted return on capital
   b. Discount factor
   c. Discounting
   d. Risk

77. In finance, a _____ is a debt security, in which the authorized issuer owes the holders a debt and, depending on the terms of the _____, is obliged to pay interest (the coupon) and/or to repay the principal at a later date, termed maturity. It is a formal contract to repay borrowed money with interest at fixed intervals.

Thus a _____ is like a loan: the issuer is the borrower, the _____ holder is the lender, and the coupon is the interest.

   a. Zero-coupon bond
   b. Revenue bonds
   c. Coupon rate
   d. Bond

78. A _____ is a party (e.g. person, organization, company, or government) that has a claim to the services of a second party. It is a person or institution to whom money is owed. The first party, in general, has provided some property or service to the second party under the assumption (usually enforced by contract) that the second party will return an equivalent property or service.
   a. Par value
   b. Treasury company
   c. Payback period
   d. Creditor

79. _____ is the amount of time someone works beyond normal working hours. Normal hours may be determined in several ways:

- by custom (what is considered healthy or reasonable by society),
- by practices of a given trade or profession,
- by legislation,
- by agreement between employers and workers or their representatives.

Most nations have _____ laws designed to dissuade or prevent employers from forcing their employees to work excessively long hours. These laws may take into account other considerations than the humanitarian, such as increasing the overall level of employment in the economy. One common approach to regulating _____ is to require employers to pay workers at a higher hourly rate for _____ work.

a. ABC Television Network
b. AMEX
c. AIG
d. Overtime

Chapter 2. Analyzing and Recording Transactions

1. The basic _____ is the foundation for the double-entry bookkeeping system. It shows how assets were financed: either by borrowing money from someone (liability) or by paying your own money (shareholders' equity.)

   Assets = Liabilities + (Shareholders or Owners equity)

For example: A student buys a computer for $945.

   a. AMEX
   b. AIG
   c. ABC Television Network
   d. Accounting equation

2. _____ is one of a series of accounting transactions dealing with the billing of customers who owe money to a person, company or organization for goods and services that have been provided to the customer. In most business entities this is typically done by generating an invoice and mailing or electronically delivering it to the customer, who in turn must pay it within an established timeframe called credit or payment terms.

An example of a common payment term is Net 30, meaning payment is due in the amount of the invoice 30 days from the date of invoice.

   a. Accrual
   b. Adjusting entries
   c. Accounts receivable
   d. Accrued revenue

3. In business and accounting, _____ are everything of value that is owned by a person or company. It is a claim on the property your income of a borrower. The balance sheet of a firm records the monetary value of the _____ owned by the firm.

   a. Accounts receivable
   b. Accrual basis accounting
   c. Earnings before interest, taxes, depreciation and amortization
   d. Assets

4. _____ is the balance of the amounts of cash being received and paid by a business during a defined period of time, sometimes tied to a specific project. Measurement of _____ can be used

   - to evaluate the state or performance of a business or project.
   - to determine problems with liquidity. Being profitable does not necessarily mean being liquid. A company can fail because of a shortage of cash, even while profitable.
   - to project rate of returns. The time of _____ s into and out of projects are used as inputs to financial models such as internal rate of return, and net present value.
   - to examine income or growth of a business when it is believed that accrual accounting concepts do not represent economic realities. Alternately, _____ can be used to 'validate' the net income generated by accrual accounting.

_____ as a generic term may be used differently depending on context, and certain _____ definitions may be adapted by analysts and users for their own uses. Common terms include operating _____ and free _____.

   a. Flow-through entity
   b. Cash flow
   c. Controlling interest
   d. Commercial paper

Chapter 2. Analyzing and Recording Transactions

5. In economics a _____ is an entity that owes a debt to someone else. The entity may be an individual, a firm, a government, a company or other legal person. The counterparty is called a creditor.
   a. Shares authorized
   b. Segregated portfolio company
   c. Debtor
   d. Fair market value

6. The _____, sometimes known as the nominal ledger, is the main accounting record of a business which uses double-entry bookkeeping. It will usually include accounts for such items as current assets, fixed assets, liabilities, revenue and expense items, gains and losses.

   The _____ is a collection of the group of accounts that supports the items shown in the major financial statements.

   a. General ledger
   b. Sales journal
   c. General journal
   d. Journal entry

7. _____ represents claims for which formal instruments of credit are issued as evidence of debt, such as a promissory note. The credit instrument normally requires the debtor to pay interest and extends for time periods of 60-90 days or longer.
   a. Notes receivable
   b. Restricted stock
   c. Moving average
   d. Public offering

8. _____ refers to services paid for in advance. Examples include tolls, pay as you go cell phones, and stored-value cards such as gift cards and preloaded credit cards. _____ accounts are assets, and they are increased by debiting the account(s.)
   a. 3M Company
   b. Prepaid
   c. BNSF Railway
   d. BMC Software, Inc.

9. _____, in accrual accounting, is any account where the asset or liability is not realized until a future date (accounting period), e.g. annuities, charges, taxes, income, etc. The _____ item may be carried, dependent on type of deferral, as either an asset or liability.
   a. Payroll
   b. Cash basis accounting
   c. Deferred
   d. Pro forma

10. A _____, also referred to as a note payable in accounting, is a contract where one party (the maker or issuer) makes an unconditional promise in writing to pay a sum of money to the other (the payee), either at a fixed or determinable future time or on demand of the payee, under specific terms. They differ from IOUs in that they contain a specific promise to pay, rather than simply acknowledging that a debt exists.

    The terms of a note typically include the principal amount, the interest rate if any, and the maturity date.

    a. BMC Software, Inc.
    b. 3M Company
    c. BNSF Railway
    d. Promissory note

11. A _____ is the pinnacle activity involved in selling products or services in return for money or other compensation. It is an act of completion of a commercial activity.

A _____ is completed by the seller, the owner of the goods.

a. Maturity
b. High yield stock
c. Tertiary sector of economy
d. Sale

12. In accounting, _____ or carrying value is the value of an asset according to its balance sheet account balance. For assets, the value is based on the original cost of the asset less any depreciation, amortization or impairment costs made against the asset. Traditionally, a company's _____ is its total assets minus intangible assets and liabilities.

a. Book value
b. Generally accepted accounting principles
c. Matching principle
d. Depreciation

13. In accounting, _____ has a very specific meaning. It is an outflow of cash or other valuable assets from a person or company to another person or company. This outflow of cash is generally one side of a trade for products or services that have equal or better current or future value to the buyer than to the seller.

a. ABC Television Network
b. AIG
c. Expense
d. AMEX

14. _____ is a file or account that contains money that a person or company owes to suppliers, but has not paid yet (a form of debt.) When you receive an invoice you add it to the file, and then you remove it when you pay. Thus, the A/P is a form of credit that suppliers offer to their purchasers by allowing them to pay for a product or service after it has already been received.

a. Accrual
b. Accounts payable
c. Earnings before interest, taxes, depreciation and amortization
d. Accounts receivable

15. A _____ is a party (e.g. person, organization, company, or government) that has a claim to the services of a second party. It is a person or institution to whom money is owed. The first party, in general, has provided some property or service to the second party under the assumption (usually enforced by contract) that the second party will return an equivalent property or service.

a. Treasury company
b. Payback period
c. Par value
d. Creditor

16. _____, in law and economics, is a form of risk management primarily used to hedge against the risk of a contingent loss. _____ is defined as the equitable transfer of the risk of a loss, from one entity to another, in exchange for a premium, and can be thought of as a guaranteed small loss to prevent a large, possibly devastating loss. An insurer is a company selling the _____; an insured is the person or entity buying the _____.

a. AMEX
b. ABC Television Network
c. AIG
d. Insurance

17. _____ are defined as identifiable non-monetary assets that cannot be seen, touched or physically measured, which are created through time and/or effort and that are identifiable as a separate asset. There are two primary forms of intangibles - legal intangibles (such as trade secrets (e.g., customer lists), copyrights, patents, trademarks, and goodwill) and competitive intangibles (such as knowledge activities (know-how, knowledge), collaboration activities, leverage activities, and structural activities.) Legal intangibles are known under the generic term intellectual property and generate legal property rights defensible in a court of law.

a. Overhead
b. ABC Television Network
c. AIG
d. Intangible assets

18. In financial accounting, a _____ is defined as an obligation of an entity arising from past transactions or events, the settlement of which may result in the transfer or use of assets, provision of services or other yielding of economic benefits in the future.
   a. Corporate governance
   b. False Claims Act
   c. Vested
   d. Liability

19. _____ is the generic term that refers to all supplies regularly used in offices by businesses and other organizations, from private citizens to governments, who works with the collection, refinement, and output of information (colloquially referred to as 'paper work'.) _____ being sold at a drugstore. Hà Ná»™i's Stationery supplier

The term includes small, expendable, daily use items such as paper clips, staples, hole punches, binders and laminators, writing utensils and paper, but also encompasses higher-cost equipment like computers, printers, fax machines, photocopiers and cash registers, as well as office furniture such as cubicles or armoire desks. Two very common medium-to-high-cost office equipment items before the advent of suitably priced word processing machines and PCs in the 1970s and 1980s were typewriters and adding machines.

   a. AIG
   b. ABC Television Network
   c. AMEX
   d. Office supplies

20. In economic models, the _____ time frame assumes no fixed factors of production. Firms can enter or leave the marketplace, and the cost (and availability) of land, labor, raw materials, and capital goods can be assumed to vary. In contrast, in the short-run time frame, certain factors are assumed to be fixed, because there is not sufficient time for them to change.
   a. Long-run
   b. Short-run
   c. BMC Software, Inc.
   d. 3M Company

21. _____, is a liability with an uncertain timing or amount, but where the uncertainty is not significant enough to qualify it as a provision. An example is an unpaid obligation to pay for goods or services received FROM a counterpart, while cash for them is to be paid out in a latter accounting period when its amount is deducted from _____s.
   a. Assets
   b. Accounts receivable
   c. Accrued expense
   d. Accrual basis accounting

22. _____ is a form of corporation equity ownership represented in the securities. It is a stock whose dividends are based on market fluctuations. It is dangerous in comparison to preferred shares and some other investment options, in that in the event of bankruptcy, _____ investors receive their funds after preferred stock holders, bondholders, creditors, etc. On the other hand, common shares on average perform better than preferred shares or bonds over time.
   a. Stock split
   b. Common stock
   c. 3M Company
   d. Growth investing

23. _____ are formal bookkeeping and accounting terms. They are the most fundamental concepts in accounting, representing the two records that one party in a transaction makes on its records, transferring a money balance from one account to another, one representing a reduction of liability or increase in asset, and the other representing a balancing increase in liability or reduction of asset.

Chapter 2. Analyzing and Recording Transactions

Debits and credits are a system of notation used in accounting to keep track of money movements (transactions) into and out of an account.

a. Bookkeeping
b. Controlling account
c. Debit and credit
d. Cookie jar accounting

24. _____ are payments made by a corporation to its shareholder members. It is the portion of corporate profits paid out to stockholders. When a corporation earns a profit or surplus, that money can be put to two uses: it can either be re-invested in the business (called retained earnings), or it can be paid to the shareholders as a dividend.

a. Dividend yield
b. Dividend payout ratio
c. Dividend stripping
d. Dividends

25. _____, in accrual accounting, (e.g. advance payment received from a client) is, according to revenue recognition, revenue not earned until the delivery of goods or services, which until then, is still owed to the payer, hence remaining a liability.

_____, sometimes referred to as deferred revenue or unearned revenue, shares characteristics with accrued expense with the difference that a liability to be covered latter is cash received FROM a counterpart, while goods or services are to be delivered in a latter period, when such income item is earned, the related revenue item is recognized, and the same amount is deducted from deferred revenues.

a. Matching principle
b. Treasury stock
c. Deferred income
d. Gross sales

26. _____ is a list of the accounts including a unique number of each allowing to locate it in each ledger. The list is typically arranged in the order of the customary appearance of accounts in the financial statements. A _____ can track a specific financial information.

a. General journal
b. General ledger
c. Journal entry
d. Chart of accounts

27. In economics, the _____, (or _____) measures the payments that flow between any individual country and all other countries. It is used to summarize all international economic transactions for that country during a specific time period, usually a year. The _____ is determined by the country's exports and imports of goods, services, and financial capital, as well as financial transfers.

a. Yield to maturity
b. Balance of payments
c. Moving average
d. Stock split

28. _____ and credit are formal bookkeeping and accounting terms. They are the most fundamental concepts in accounting, representing the two records that one party in a transaction makes on its records, transferring a money balance from one account to another, one representing a reduction of liability or increase in asset, and the other representing a balancing increase in liability or reduction of asset.

Introduction

Chapter 2. Analyzing and Recording Transactions

_____s and credits are a system of notation used in accounting to keep track of money movements (transactions) into and out of an account.

- a. Debit and credit
- b. Debit
- c. Bookkeeping
- d. Cookie jar accounting

29. _____ is a system of financial accounting where each transaction is recorded in at least two accounts: at least one account is debited and at least one account is credited, so that the total debits of the transaction equal to the total credits. For example, if Company A sells an item to Company B, and Company B pays by cheque, then the bookkeeper of Company A credits the account 'Sales' and debits the account 'Bank'. Conversely, the bookkeeper of Company B debits the account 'Purchases' and credits the account 'Bank'.

- a. Bookkeeping
- b. Cookie jar accounting
- c. Debit and credit
- d. Double-entry bookkeeping

30. The term _____, derived from the distinctive T shape, is frequently used when discussing or analyzing accounting or business transactions. _____s are used to represent general ledger accounts.

Typically one or more Ts are drawn on a white board or blank piece of paper. A general ledger account name or number is then written above each T. Debit entries are recorded on the left side of the 'T' and credit entries are recorded on the right side of the 'T'.

- a. BNSF Railway
- b. BMC Software, Inc.
- c. 3M Company
- d. T account

31. The _____ is where double entry bookkeeping entries are recorded by debiting one account and crediting another account with the same amount. The amount debited and the amount credited should always be equal, thereby ensuring the accounting equation is maintained.

Depending on the business's accounting information system, specialized journals may be used in conjunction with the _____ for record-keeping.

- a. Journal entry
- b. General ledger
- c. Sales journal
- d. General journal

32. A _____ has several related meanings:

- a daily record of events or business; a private _____ is usually referred to as a diary.
- a newspaper or other periodical, in the literal sense of one published each day;
- many publications issued at stated intervals, such as magazines, or scholarly academic _____s, or the record of the transactions of a society, are often called _____s. Although _____ is sometimes used, erroneously, as a synonym for 'magazine,' in academic use, a _____ refers to a serious, scholarly publication, most often peer-reviewed. A non-scholarly magazine written for an educated audience about an industry or an area of professional activity is usually called a professional magazine.

The word 'journalist' for one whose business is writing for the public press has been in use since the end of the 17th century.

Open access _____s are scholarly _____s that are available to the reader without financial or other barrier other than access to the internet itself. Some are subsidized, and some require payment on behalf of the author. Subsidized _____s are financed by an academic institution or a government information center.

   a. BMC Software, Inc.
   c. 3M Company
   b. BNSF Railway
   d. Journal

33. The _____ of 2002 (Pub.L. 107-204, 116 Stat. 745, enacted July 30, 2002), also known as the Public Company Accounting Reform and Investor Protection Act of 2002, is a United States federal law enacted on July 30, 2002 in response to a number of major corporate and accounting scandals including those affecting Enron, Tyco International, Adelphia, Peregrine Systems and WorldCom. The legislation establishes new or enhanced standards for all U.S. public company boards, management, and public accounting firms. It does not apply to privately held companies.
   a. Lease
   c. Fair Labor Standards Act
   b. Sarbanes-Oxley Act
   d. FCPA

34. _____ is application software that records and processes accounting transactions within functional modules such as accounts payable, accounts receivable, payroll, and trial balance. It functions as an accounting information system. It may be developed in-house by the company or organization using it, may be purchased from a third party, or may be a combination of a third-party application software package with local modifications.
   a. Amgen
   c. Economic value added
   b. AIG
   d. Accounting software

35. _____ is the recording of the value of assets, liabilities, income, and expenses in the daybooks, journals, and ledgers, in which debit and credit entries are chronologically posted to record changes in value. _____ is often mistaken for accounting, which is the system of recording, verifying, and reporting such information. Practitioners of accounting are called accountants.
   a. Bookkeeping
   c. Debit and credit
   b. Double-entry bookkeeping
   d. Controlling account

36. _____ refers to a business or organization attempting to acquire goods or services to accomplish the goals of the enterprise. Though there are several organizations that attempt to set standards in the _____ process, processes can vary greatly between organizations. Typically the word e;_____e; is not used interchangeably with the word e;procuremente;, since procurement typically includes Expediting, Supplier Quality, and Traffic and Logistics (T'L) in addition to _____.
   a. Supply chain
   c. Consignor
   b. Purchasing
   d. Free port

37. A _____ is the transfer of wealth from one party (such as a person or company) to another. A _____ is usually made in exchange for the provision of goods, services or both, or to fulfill a legal obligation.

The simplest and oldest form of _____ is barter, the exchange of one good or service for another.

a. 3M Company
c. BMC Software, Inc.
b. Payee
d. Payment

38. A _____ is a compensation, usually financial, received by a worker in exchange for their labor.

Compensation in terms of _____s is given to worker and compensation in terms of salary is given to employees. Compensation is a monetary benefits given to employees in returns of the services provided by them.

a. 3M Company
c. BMC Software, Inc.
b. Retirement plan
d. Wage

39. _____ is the term used to refer to the standard framework of guidelines for financial accounting used in any given jurisdiction. _____ includes the standards, conventions, and rules accountants follow in recording and summarizing transactions, and in the preparation of financial statements.

Financial accounting information must be assembled and reported objectively.

a. Long-term liabilities
c. General ledger
b. Current asset
d. Generally accepted accounting principles

40. _____ principle is a cornerstone of accrual accounting together with matching principle. They both determine the accounting period, in which revenues and expenses are recognized. According to the principle, revenues are recognized when they are (1) realized or realizable, and are (2) earned (usually when goods are transferred or services rendered), no matter when cash is received.

a. 3M Company
c. BMC Software, Inc.
b. Revenue recognition
d. Net realizable value

41. A _____, in accounting, is a logging of transcriptions into items accounting journal. The _____ can consist of several items, each of which is either a debit or a credit. The total of the debits must equal the total of the credits, or the _____ is said to be 'unbalanced.' Journal entries can record unique items or recurring items such as depreciation or bond amortization.

a. Sales journal
c. General journal
b. General ledger
d. Journal entry

42. _____ is a company's financial statement that indicates how the revenue is transformed into the net income The purpose of the _____ is to show managers and investors whether the company made or lost money during the period being reported.

The important thing to remember about an _____ is that it represents a period of time.

a. Income statement
c. AMEX
b. ABC Television Network
d. AIG

Chapter 2. Analyzing and Recording Transactions

43. In accounting, the _____ is a worksheet listing the balance at a certain date, of each ledger account in two columns, namely debit and credit. Under the double-entry system, in any transaction the total of any debits must equal the total of any credits, so in a _____ the total of the debit side should always be equal to the total of the credit side. The _____ thus serves as a tool to detect errors, which can result in the totals not being equal.
   a. Depreciation
   b. Current asset
   c. Bottom line
   d. Trial balance

44. An _____ is a term used in behavioral economics to describe those types of behaviors that impose costs on a person in the long-run that are not taken into account when making decisions in the present. Classical Economics discourages government from creating legislation that targets internalities, because it is assumed that the consumer takes these personal costs into account when paying for the good that causes the _____. For example, cigarettes should be taxed because of the negative consumption externalities that they impose, such as second-hand smoke, not because the smoker harms him or herself by smoking.
   a. Inventory turnover ratio
   b. Operating budget
   c. Authorised capital
   d. Internality

45. The _____ is the United States federal government agency that collects taxes and enforces the internal revenue laws. It is an agency within the U.S. Dept of the treasury responsible for interpretation and application of Federal tax law. The official U.S. Treasury regulations provide (in part):

The _____ is a bureau of the Department of the Treasury under the immediate direction of the Commissioner of Internal Revenue.

   a. Income tax
   b. Use tax
   c. Indirect tax
   d. Internal Revenue Service

46. _____ are formal records of a business' financial activities.

In British English, including United Kingdom company law, _____ are often referred to as accounts, although the term _____ is also used, particularly by accountants.

_____ provide an overview of a business' financial condition in both short and long term.

   a. Statement of retained earnings
   b. Notes to the financial statements
   c. 3M Company
   d. Financial statements

47. In financial accounting, a _____ or statement of financial position is a summary of a person's or organization's balances. Assets, liabilities and ownership equity are listed as of a specific date, such as the end of its financial year. A _____ is often described as a snapshot of a company's financial condition.
   a. Financial statements
   b. Statement of retained earnings
   c. Balance sheet
   d. 3M Company

Chapter 2. Analyzing and Recording Transactions

48. The term _____ refers to government debt, expenditures and revenues, or to finance (particularly financial revenue) in general.

- _____ deficit is the budget deficit of federal or local government
- _____ policy is the discretionary spending of governments. Contrasts with monetary policy.
- _____ year and _____ quarter are reporting periods for firms and other agencies.

See also

- Procurator _____ and Crown Office and Procurator _____ Service

a. Comparable

b. Scientific Research and Experimental Development Tax Incentive Program

c. Swap

d. Fiscal

49. A _____ is a period used for calculating annual financial statements in businesses and other organizations. In many jurisdictions, regulatory laws regarding accounting and taxation require such reports once per twelve months, but do not require that the period reported on constitutes a calendar year (i.e., January through December.) _____s vary between businesses and countries.

a. BNSF Railway
b. BMC Software, Inc.
c. 3M Company
d. Fiscal year

50. A _____ is a computer application that simulates a paper worksheet. It displays multiple cells that together make up a grid consisting of rows and columns, each cell containing either alphanumeric text or numeric values. A _____ cell may alternatively contain a formula that defines how the contents of that cell is to be calculated from the contents of any other cell (or combination of cells) each time any cell is updated.

a. Merck ' Co., Inc.
b. Spreadsheet
c. Linear regression
d. Mutual fund

51. _____ is a specific term used in companies' financial reporting from the company-whole point of view. Because that use excludes the effects of changing ownership interest, an economic measure of _____ is necessary for financial analysis from the shareholders' point of view

_____ is defined by the Financial Accounting Standards Board, or FASB, as 'the change in equity [net assets] of a business enterprise during a period from transactions and other events and circumstances from nonowner sources. It includes all changes in equity during a period except those resulting from investments by owners and distributions to owners.'

_____ is the sum of net income and other items that must bypass the income statement because they have not been realized, including items like an unrealized holding gain or loss from available for sale securities and foreign currency translation gains or losses.

a. 3M Company
b. BMC Software, Inc.
c. BNSF Railway
d. Comprehensive income

52. The _____ is one of the basic financial statements as per Generally Accepted Accounting Principles, and it explains the changes in a company's retained earnings over the reporting period. It breaks down changes affecting the account, such as profits or losses from operations, dividends paid, and any other items charged or credited to retained earnings. A retained earnings statement is required by Generally Accepted Accounting Principles whenever comparative balance sheets and income statements are presented.
   a. Financial statements
   b. Statement of retained earnings
   c. 3M Company
   d. Notes to the financial statements

53. _____ is that which is owed; usually referencing assets owed, but the term can also cover moral obligations and other interactions not requiring money. In the case of assets, _____ is a means of using future purchasing power in the present before a summation has been earned. Some companies and corporations use _____ as a part of their overall corporate finance strategy.
   a. Lender
   b. Debenture
   c. Debt
   d. Loan

54. _____ is a financial ratio that indicates the percentage of a company's assets are provided via debt. It is the ratio of total debt (the sum of current liabilities and long-term liabilities) and total assets (the sum of current assets, fixed assets, and other assets such as 'goodwill'.)

$$\text{Debt ratio} = \frac{\text{Total Debt}}{\text{Total Assets}}$$

or alternatively:

$$\text{Debt ratio} = \frac{\text{Total Liability}}{\text{Total Assets}}$$

For example, a company with $2 million in total assets and $500,000 in total liabilities would have a _____ of 25%

Like all financial ratios, a company's _____ should be compared with their industry average or other competing firms.

   a. 3M Company
   b. Finance lease
   c. Profitability index
   d. Debt ratio

1. An _____ is a period with reference to which United Kingdom corporation tax is charged. It helps dictate when tax is paid on income and gains. An _____ begins whenever a company comes within the corporation tax charge, and whenever an _____ ends without the company ceasing to be within the charge.
   a. AMEX
   b. ABC Television Network
   c. AIG
   d. Accounting period

2. _____ is the term used to refer to the standard framework of guidelines for financial accounting used in any given jurisdiction. _____ includes the standards, conventions, and rules accountants follow in recording and summarizing transactions, and in the preparation of financial statements.

   Financial accounting information must be assembled and reported objectively.

   a. Current asset
   b. Long-term liabilities
   c. Generally accepted accounting principles
   d. General ledger

3. _____ are formal records of a business' financial activities.

   In British English, including United Kingdom company law, _____ are often referred to as accounts, although the term _____ is also used, particularly by accountants.

   _____ provide an overview of a business' financial condition in both short and long term.

   a. 3M Company
   b. Notes to the financial statements
   c. Statement of retained earnings
   d. Financial statements

4. _____ of something is, in finance, the adding together of interest or different investments over a period of time such as atoms (1 - the act or process of accruing; 2 - the amount that accrues.) It holds specific meanings in accounting and payroll.

   _____, in accounting, describes the accounting method known as _____ basis, whereby revenues and expenses are recognized when they are accrued, i.e. accumulated (earned or incurred), regardless when the actual cash is received or paid out.

   a. Earnings before interest, taxes, depreciation and amortization
   b. Accounts receivable
   c. Assets
   d. Accrual

5. _____ is a method of accounting whereby economic activities (rather than cash flow) of financial events are considered, because of two complementary principles, which (together) determine the point, at which expenses and revenues are recognized. According to revenue recognition principle, revenues are realized when earned, whether or not they are received in cash.
   a. Accrued revenue
   b. Accrual
   c. Earnings before interest, taxes, depreciation and amortization
   d. Accrual basis accounting

Chapter 3. Adjusting Accounts and Preparing Financial Statements

6. _____ is a method of accounting whereby cash flow of financial events is considered. The method recognizes revenues when cash is received and recognizes expenses when cash is paid out. In cash accounting, revenues and expenses are also called cash receipts and cash payments respectively.

   a. Closing entries
   b. Net sales
   c. Cash basis accounting
   d. Treasury stock

7. In accounting, _____ has a very specific meaning. It is an outflow of cash or other valuable assets from a person or company to another person or company. This outflow of cash is generally one side of a trade for products or services that have equal or better current or future value to the buyer than to the seller.

   a. ABC Television Network
   b. AIG
   c. AMEX
   d. Expense

8. The term _____ refers to government debt, expenditures and revenues, or to finance (particularly financial revenue) in general.

   - _____ deficit is the budget deficit of federal or local government
   - _____ policy is the discretionary spending of governments. Contrasts with monetary policy.
   - _____ year and _____ quarter are reporting periods for firms and other agencies.

   See also

   - Procurator _____ and Crown Office and Procurator _____ Service

   a. Swap
   b. Scientific Research and Experimental Development Tax Incentive Program
   c. Comparable
   d. Fiscal

9. A _____ is a period used for calculating annual financial statements in businesses and other organizations. In many jurisdictions, regulatory laws regarding accounting and taxation require such reports once per twelve months, but do not require that the period reported on constitutes a calendar year (i.e., January through December.) _____s vary between businesses and countries.

   a. Fiscal year
   b. BNSF Railway
   c. BMC Software, Inc.
   d. 3M Company

10. A _____ is the pinnacle activity involved in selling products or services in return for money or other compensation. It is an act of completion of a commercial activity.

    A _____ is completed by the seller, the owner of the goods.

    a. High yield stock
    b. Maturity
    c. Tertiary sector of economy
    d. Sale

Chapter 3. Adjusting Accounts and Preparing Financial Statements

11. A _____ is a computer application that simulates a paper worksheet. It displays multiple cells that together make up a grid consisting of rows and columns, each cell containing either alphanumeric text or numeric values. A _____ cell may alternatively contain a formula that defines how the contents of that cell is to be calculated from the contents of any other cell (or combination of cells) each time any cell is updated.
   a. Merck ' Co., Inc.
   b. Spreadsheet
   c. Linear regression
   d. Mutual fund

12. _____ is a fee paid on borrowed assets. It is the price paid for the use of borrowed money, or, money earned by deposited funds. Assets that are sometimes lent with _____ include money, shares, consumer goods through hire purchase, major assets such as aircraft, and even entire factories in finance lease arrangements. The _____ is calculated upon the value of the assets in the same manner as upon money.
   a. Insolvency
   b. ABC Television Network
   c. AIG
   d. Interest

13. _____ refers to services paid for in advance. Examples include tolls, pay as you go cell phones, and stored-value cards such as gift cards and preloaded credit cards. _____ accounts are assets, and they are increased by debiting the account(s.)
   a. Prepaid
   b. BMC Software, Inc.
   c. 3M Company
   d. BNSF Railway

14. _____, in accrual accounting, is any account where the asset or liability is not realized until a future date (accounting period), e.g. annuities, charges, taxes, income, etc. The _____ item may be carried, dependent on type of deferral, as either an asset or liability.
   a. Cash basis accounting
   b. Payroll
   c. Pro forma
   d. Deferred

15. In accounting/accountancy, _____ are journal entries usually made at the end of an accounting period to allocate income and expenditure to the period in which they actually occurred. The revenue recognition principle is the basis of making _____ that pertain to unearned and accrued revenues under accrual-basis accounting. They are sometimes called Balance Day adjustments because they are made on balance day.
   a. Accrued expense
   b. Accrual
   c. Earnings before interest, taxes, depreciation and amortization
   d. Adjusting entries

16. The Federal National Mortgage Association (FNMA) (NYSE: FNM), commonly known as _____, is a stockholder-owned corporation chartered by Congress in 1968 as a government sponsored enterprise (GSE), but founded in 1938 during the Great Depression. The corporation's purpose is to purchase and securitize mortgages in order to ensure that funds are consistently available to the institutions that lend money to home buyers.

On September 7, 2008, James Lockhart, director of the Federal Housing Finance Agency (FHFA), announced that _____ and Freddie Mac were being placed into conservatorship of the FHFA.

   a. National Conference of Commissioners on Uniform State Laws
   b. Freddie Mac
   c. Public company
   d. Fannie Mae

Chapter 3. Adjusting Accounts and Preparing Financial Statements 31

17. _____ is a cornerstone of accrual accounting together with the revenue recognition principle. They both determine the accounting period, in which revenues and expenses are recognized. According to the principle, expenses are recognized when obligations are (1) incurred (usually when goods are transferred or services rendered, e.g. sold), and (2) offset against recognized revenues, which were generated from those expenses (related on the cause-and-effect basis), no matter when cash is paid out.

a. Net sales
b. Payroll
c. Matching principle
d. Current liabilities

18. _____ principle is a cornerstone of accrual accounting together with matching principle. They both determine the accounting period, in which revenues and expenses are recognized. According to the principle, revenues are recognized when they are (1) realized or realizable, and are (2) earned (usually when goods are transferred or services rendered), no matter when cash is received.

a. Net realizable value
b. BMC Software, Inc.
c. 3M Company
d. Revenue recognition

19. The _____ of 2002 (Pub.L. 107-204, 116 Stat. 745, enacted July 30, 2002), also known as the Public Company Accounting Reform and Investor Protection Act of 2002, is a United States federal law enacted on July 30, 2002 in response to a number of major corporate and accounting scandals including those affecting Enron, Tyco International, Adelphia, Peregrine Systems and WorldCom. The legislation establishes new or enhanced standards for all U.S. public company boards, management, and public accounting firms. It does not apply to privately held companies.

a. Lease
b. Sarbanes-Oxley Act
c. Fair Labor Standards Act
d. FCPA

20. _____, in law and economics, is a form of risk management primarily used to hedge against the risk of a contingent loss. _____ is defined as the equitable transfer of the risk of a loss, from one entity to another, in exchange for a premium, and can be thought of as a guaranteed small loss to prevent a large, possibly devastating loss. An insurer is a company selling the _____; an insured is the person or entity buying the _____.

a. AMEX
b. AIG
c. Insurance
d. ABC Television Network

21. _____ is a term used in accounting, economics and finance to spread the cost of an asset over the span of several years.

In simple words we can say that _____ is the reduction in the value of an asset due to usage, passage of time, wear and tear, technological outdating or obsolescence, depletion, inadequacy, rot, rust, decay or other such factors.

In accounting, _____ is a term used to describe any method of attributing the historical or purchase cost of an asset across its useful life, roughly corresponding to normal wear and tear.

a. General ledger
b. Net profit
c. Current asset
d. Depreciation

22. In business and accounting, _____ are everything of value that is owned by a person or company. It is a claim on the property your income of a borrower. The balance sheet of a firm records the monetary value of the _____ owned by the firm.

a. Accrual basis accounting

b. Earnings before interest, taxes, depreciation and amortization

c. Accounts receivable

d. Assets

23. Book Value = Original Cost - _____

Book value at the end of year becomes book value at the beginning of next year. The asset is depreciated until the book value equals scrap value.

If the vehicle were to be sold and the sales price exceeded the depreciated value (net book value) then the excess would be considered a gain and subject to depreciation recapture.

a. AMEX
b. AIG
c. ABC Television Network
d. Accumulated depreciation

24. In accounting, _____ or carrying value is the value of an asset according to its balance sheet account balance. For assets, the value is based on the original cost of the asset less any depreciation, amortization or impairment costs made against the asset. Traditionally, a company's _____ is its total assets minus intangible assets and liabilities.

a. Generally accepted accounting principles
b. Matching principle
c. Depreciation
d. Book value

25. _____ are formal bookkeeping and accounting terms. They are the most fundamental concepts in accounting, representing the two records that one party in a transaction makes on its records, transferring a money balance from one account to another, one representing a reduction of liability or increase in asset, and the other representing a balancing increase in liability or reduction of asset.

Debits and credits are a system of notation used in accounting to keep track of money movements (transactions) into and out of an account.

a. Controlling account
b. Cookie jar accounting
c. Bookkeeping
d. Debit and credit

26. In economics, business, retail, and accounting, a _____ is the value of money that has been used up to produce something, and hence is not available for use anymore. In economics, a _____ is an alternative that is given up as a result of a decision. In business, the _____ may be one of acquisition, in which case the amount of money expended to acquire it is counted as _____.

a. Cost
b. Cost of quality
c. Cost allocation
d. Prime cost

27. _____ was a maxim coined by Josiah Warren, indicating a (prescriptive) version of the labor theory of value. Warren maintained that the just compensation for labor (or for its product) could only be an equivalent amount of labor (or a product embodying an equivalent amount.) Thus, profit, rent, and interest were considered unjust economic arrangements.

a. Politicized issue
b. 3M Company
c. BMC Software, Inc.
d. Cost the limit of price

Chapter 3. Adjusting Accounts and Preparing Financial Statements

28. Straight-line depreciation is the simplest and most often used technique, in which the company estimates the _____ of the asset at the end of the period during which it will be used to generate revenues (useful life), and will expense a portion of original cost in equal increments over that period. The _____ is an estimate of the value of the asset at the time it will be sold or disposed of; it may be zero. _____ is scrap value, by another name.
   a. Generally accepted accounting principles
   b. Closing entries
   c. Net profit
   d. Salvage value

29. There are several methods for calculating depreciation, generally based on either the passage of time or the level of activity (or use) of the asset.

   _____ is the simplest and most often used technique, in which the company estimates the salvage value of the asset at the end of the period during which it will be used to generate revenues (useful life), and will expense a portion of original cost in equal increments over that period.

   a. Closing entries
   b. Straight-line depreciation
   c. Current asset
   d. Pro forma

30. The _____ is a business model where a customer must pay a subscription price to have access to the product/service. The model was pioneered by magazines and newspapers, but is now used by many businesses and websites. Rather than selling products individually, a subscription sells periodic (monthly or yearly or seasonal) use or access to a product or service, or, in the case of such non-profit organizations as opera companies or symphony orchestras, it sells tickets to the entire run of five to fifteen scheduled performances for an entire season.
   a. BMC Software, Inc.
   b. 3M Company
   c. BNSF Railway
   d. Subscription business model

31. _____, in accrual accounting, (e.g. advance payment received from a client) is, according to revenue recognition, revenue not earned until the delivery of goods or services, which until then, is still owed to the payer, hence remaining a liability.

   _____, sometimes referred to as deferred revenue or unearned revenue, shares characteristics with accrued expense with the difference that a liability to be covered latter is cash received FROM a counterpart, while goods or services are to be delivered in a latter period, when such income item is earned, the related revenue item is recognized, and the same amount is deducted from deferred revenues.

   a. Deferred income
   b. Gross sales
   c. Treasury stock
   d. Matching principle

32. _____, is a liability with an uncertain timing or amount, but where the uncertainty is not significant enough to qualify it as a provision. An example is an unpaid obligation to pay for goods or services received FROM a counterpart, while cash for them is to be paid out in a latter accounting period when its amount is deducted from _____s.
   a. Accrued expense
   b. Assets
   c. Accounts receivable
   d. Accrual basis accounting

33. _____ consists of the sale of goods or merchandise from a fixed location, such as a department store, boutique or kiosk in small or individual lots for direct consumption by the purchaser. _____ may include subordinated services, such as delivery. Purchasers may be individuals or businesses.

a. BMC Software, Inc.
b. 3M Company
c. Retailing
d. BNSF Railway

34. _____ relates to the cost of borrowing money. It is the price that a lender charges a borrower for the use of the lender's money. _____ is different from OPEX and CAPEX, for it relates to the capital structure of a company.
   a. ABC Television Network
   b. Interest expense
   c. Interest
   d. AIG

35. A _____ is the transfer of wealth from one party (such as a person or company) to another. A _____ is usually made in exchange for the provision of goods, services or both, or to fulfill a legal obligation.

The simplest and oldest form of _____ is barter, the exchange of one good or service for another.

   a. 3M Company
   b. BMC Software, Inc.
   c. Payment
   d. Payee

36. _____ is a file or account that contains money that a person or company owes to suppliers, but has not paid yet (a form of debt.) When you receive an invoice you add it to the file, and then you remove it when you pay. Thus, the A/P is a form of credit that suppliers offer to their purchasers by allowing them to pay for a product or service after it has already been received.
   a. Accounts receivable
   b. Earnings before interest, taxes, depreciation and amortization
   c. Accrual
   d. Accounts payable

37. _____ is an asset, such as unpaid proceeds from a delivery of goods or services, at which such income item is earned and the related revenue item is recognized, while cash for them is to be received in a latter period, when its amount is deducted from the _____.
   a. Assets
   b. Accrued expense
   c. Accounts receivable
   d. Accrued revenue

38. In economics a _____ is an entity that owes a debt to someone else. The entity may be an individual, a firm, a government, a company or other legal person. The counterparty is called a creditor.
   a. Fair market value
   b. Segregated portfolio company
   c. Shares authorized
   d. Debtor

39. _____ is one of a series of accounting transactions dealing with the billing of customers who owe money to a person, company or organization for goods and services that have been provided to the customer. In most business entities this is typically done by generating an invoice and mailing or electronically delivering it to the customer, who in turn must pay it within an established timeframe called credit or payment terms.

An example of a common payment term is Net 30, meaning payment is due in the amount of the invoice 30 days from the date of invoice.

   a. Adjusting entries
   b. Accrued revenue
   c. Accrual
   d. Accounts receivable

40. In accounting, the _____ is a worksheet listing the balance at a certain date, of each ledger account in two columns, namely debit and credit. Under the double-entry system, in any transaction the total of any debits must equal the total of any credits, so in a _____ the total of the debit side should always be equal to the total of the credit side. The _____ thus serves as a tool to detect errors, which can result in the totals not being equal.

   a. Bottom line
   b. Depreciation
   c. Current asset
   d. Trial balance

41. In financial accounting, a _____ or statement of financial position is a summary of a person's or organization's balances. Assets, liabilities and ownership equity are listed as of a specific date, such as the end of its financial year. A _____ is often described as a snapshot of a company's financial condition.

   a. Balance sheet
   b. Financial statements
   c. 3M Company
   d. Statement of retained earnings

42. _____ is a company's financial statement that indicates how the revenue is transformed into the net income The purpose of the _____ is to show managers and investors whether the company made or lost money during the period being reported.

   The important thing to remember about an _____ is that it represents a period of time.

   a. AIG
   b. AMEX
   c. ABC Television Network
   d. Income statement

43. The term _____ is a term applied to practices that are perfunctory, or seek to satisfy the minimum requirements or to conform to a convention or doctrine. It has different meanings in different fields.

   In accounting, _____ earnings are those earnings of companies in addition to actual earnings calculated under the Generally Accepted Accounting Principles (GAAP) in their quarterly and yearly financial reports.

   a. Payroll
   b. Bottom line
   c. Treasury stock
   d. Pro forma

44. _____ is a specific term used in companies' financial reporting from the company-whole point of view. Because that use excludes the effects of changing ownership interest, an economic measure of _____ is necessary for financial analysis from the shareholders' point of view

   _____ is defined by the Financial Accounting Standards Board, or FASB, as 'the change in equity [net assets] of a business enterprise during a period from transactions and other events and circumstances from nonowner sources. It includes all changes in equity during a period except those resulting from investments by owners and distributions to owners.'

   _____ is the sum of net income and other items that must bypass the income statement because they have not been realized, including items like an unrealized holding gain or loss from available for sale securities and foreign currency translation gains or losses.

a. 3M Company
b. Comprehensive income
c. BMC Software, Inc.
d. BNSF Railway

45. The _____ is one of the basic financial statements as per Generally Accepted Accounting Principles, and it explains the changes in a company's retained earnings over the reporting period. It breaks down changes affecting the account, such as profits or losses from operations, dividends paid, and any other items charged or credited to retained earnings. A retained earnings statement is required by Generally Accepted Accounting Principles whenever comparative balance sheets and income statements are presented.
   a. Statement of retained earnings
   b. Notes to the financial statements
   c. 3M Company
   d. Financial statements

46. _____ are journal entries made at the end of an accounting period to transfer temporary accounts to permanent accounts. An 'income summary' account may be used to show the balance between revenue and expenses, or they could be directly closed against retained earnings where dividend payments will be deducted from. This process is used to reset the balance of these temporary accounts to zero for the next accounting period.
   a. FIFO and LIFO accounting
   b. Closing entries
   c. Treasury stock
   d. Trial balance

47. _____ and credit are formal bookkeeping and accounting terms. They are the most fundamental concepts in accounting, representing the two records that one party in a transaction makes on its records, transferring a money balance from one account to another, one representing a reduction of liability or increase in asset, and the other representing a balancing increase in liability or reduction of asset.

Introduction

_____s and credits are a system of notation used in accounting to keep track of money movements (transactions) into and out of an account.

   a. Debit and credit
   b. Debit
   c. Bookkeeping
   d. Cookie jar accounting

48. _____ are payments made by a corporation to its shareholder members. It is the portion of corporate profits paid out to stockholders. When a corporation earns a profit or surplus, that money can be put to two uses: it can either be re-invested in the business (called retained earnings), or it can be paid to the shareholders as a dividend.
   a. Dividend stripping
   b. Dividend yield
   c. Dividends
   d. Dividend payout ratio

49. _____ is application software that records and processes accounting transactions within functional modules such as accounts payable, accounts receivable, payroll, and trial balance. It functions as an accounting information system. It may be developed in-house by the company or organization using it, may be purchased from a third party, or may be a combination of a third-party application software package with local modifications.
   a. Amgen
   b. AIG
   c. Economic value added
   d. Accounting software

Chapter 3. Adjusting Accounts and Preparing Financial Statements

50. The _____, sometimes known as the nominal ledger, is the main accounting record of a business which uses double-entry bookkeeping. It will usually include accounts for such items as current assets, fixed assets, liabilities, revenue and expense items, gains and losses.

The _____ is a collection of the group of accounts that supports the items shown in the major financial statements.

- a. Sales journal
- b. General ledger
- c. Journal entry
- d. General journal

51. An _____ invented by esteemed professor Karen Osterheld is the system of records a business keeps to maintain its accounting system. This includes the purchase, sales, and other financial processes of the business. The purpose of an _____ is to accumulate data and provide decision makers (investors, creditors, and managers) with information to make decision While this was previously a paper-based process, most modern businesses now use accounting software such as UBS, MYOB etc.

- a. AIG
- b. Accounting information system
- c. AMEX
- d. ABC Television Network

52. In accounting, a _____ is an asset on the balance sheet which is expected to be sold or otherwise used up in the near future, usually within one year, or one business cycle - whichever is longer. Typical _____s include cash, cash equivalents, accounts receivable, inventory, the portion of prepaid accounts which will be used within a year, and short-term investments.

On the balance sheet, assets will typically be classified into _____s and long-term assets.

- a. Current asset
- b. Pro forma
- c. Deferred
- d. General ledger

53. In accounting, _____ are considered liabilities of the business that are to be settled in cash within the fiscal year or the operating cycle, whichever period is longer.

For example accounts payable for goods, services or supplies that were purchased for use in the operation of the business and payable within a normal period of time would be _____.

Bonds, mortgages and loans that are payable over a term exceeding one year would be fixed liabilities.

- a. Payroll
- b. Closing entries
- c. Treasury stock
- d. Current liabilities

54. _____ are defined as identifiable non-monetary assets that cannot be seen, touched or physically measured, which are created through time and/or effort and that are identifiable as a separate asset. There are two primary forms of intangibles - legal intangibles (such as trade secrets (e.g., customer lists), copyrights, patents, trademarks, and goodwill) and competitive intangibles (such as knowledge activities (know-how, knowledge), collaboration activities, leverage activities, and structural activities.) Legal intangibles are known under the generic term intellectual property and generate legal property rights defensible in a court of law.

Chapter 3. Adjusting Accounts and Preparing Financial Statements

a. ABC Television Network
b. Intangible assets
c. Overhead
d. AIG

55. In economic models, the _____ time frame assumes no fixed factors of production. Firms can enter or leave the marketplace, and the cost (and availability) of land, labor, raw materials, and capital goods can be assumed to vary. In contrast, in the short-run time frame, certain factors are assumed to be fixed, because there is not sufficient time for them to change.
a. 3M Company
b. Short-run
c. BMC Software, Inc.
d. Long-run

56. _____ are liabilities with a future benefit over one year, such as notes payable that mature greater than one year.

In accounting, the _____ are shown on the right wing of the balance-sheet representing the sources of funds, which are generally bounded in form of capital assets.

Examples of _____ are debentures, mortgage loans and other bank loans (note: not all bank loans are long term as not all are paid over a period greater than a year, the example is bridging loan.)

a. Gross sales
b. Long-term liabilities
c. Book value
d. Cash basis accounting

57. In finance, a _____ is a debt security, in which the authorized issuer owes the holders a debt and, depending on the terms of the _____, is obliged to pay interest (the coupon) and/or to repay the principal at a later date, termed maturity. It is a formal contract to repay borrowed money with interest at fixed intervals.

Thus a _____ is like a loan: the issuer is the borrower, the _____ holder is the lender, and the coupon is the interest.

a. Coupon rate
b. Revenue bonds
c. Bond
d. Zero-coupon bond

58. In financial accounting, a _____ is defined as an obligation of an entity arising from past transactions or events, the settlement of which may result in the transfer or use of assets, provision of services or other yielding of economic benefits in the future.
a. Liability
b. Corporate governance
c. Vested
d. False Claims Act

59. The _____ is a financial ratio that measures whether or not a firm has enough resources to pay its debts over the next 12 months. It compares a firm's current assets to its current liabilities. It is expressed as follows:

$$\text{Current ratio} = \frac{\text{Current Assets}}{\text{Current Liabilities}}$$

For example, if WXY Company's current assets are $50,000,000 and its current liabilities are $40,000,000, then its _____ would be $50,000,000 divided by $40,000,000, which equals 1.25.

Chapter 3. Adjusting Accounts and Preparing Financial Statements

a. Return on capital
b. Net Interest Income
c. Times interest earned
d. Current ratio

60. _____ is a business, economics or investment term that refers to an asset's ability to be easily converted through an act of buying or selling without causing a significant movement in the price and with minimum loss of value. Money, or cash on hand, is the most liquid asset. An act of exchange of a less liquid asset with a more liquid asset is called liquidation.

a. Financial instruments
b. Market liquidity
c. Transfer agent
d. Spot rate

61. The _____, a ratio that is typically applied to banks, in simple terms is defined as expenses as a percentage of revenue (expenses / revenue), with a few variations. A lower percentage is better since that means expenses are low and earnings are high. It is related to operating leverage, which measures the ratio between fixed costs and variable costs.

a. Average rate of return
b. Equity ratio
c. Operating leverage
d. Efficiency ratio

62. _____, net margin, net _____ or net profit ratio all refer to a measure of profitability. It is calculated by finding the net profit as a percentage of the revenue.

$$\text{Net profit margin} = \frac{\text{Net profit (after taxes)}}{\text{Revenue}} \times 100$$

The _____ is mostly used for internal comparison.

a. BMC Software, Inc.
b. Profit margin
c. BNSF Railway
d. 3M Company

63. A _____ is a piece of paper, often preprinted in a way designed to help organize material for learning or clear understanding. Students in a school may have 'fill-in-the-blank' sheets of questions, diagrams or maps to help them with their exercises. Students will often use _____s to review what has been taught in class.

a. 3M Company
b. BMC Software, Inc.
c. Value based pricing
d. Worksheet

Chapter 4. Reporting and Analyzing Merchandising Operations

1. _____ refers to the methods, practices and operations conducted to promote and sustain certain categories of commercial activity. The term is understood to have different specific meanings depending on the context. Merchandise is a sale goods at a store

In marketing, one of the definitions of _____ is the practice in which the brand or image from one product or service is used to sell another.

- a. Merchandising
- b. BMC Software, Inc.
- c. Merchandise
- d. 3M Company

2. A _____ is the pinnacle activity involved in selling products or services in return for money or other compensation. It is an act of completion of a commercial activity.

A _____ is completed by the seller, the owner of the goods.

- a. Maturity
- b. High yield stock
- c. Tertiary sector of economy
- d. Sale

3. In economics, business, retail, and accounting, a _____ is the value of money that has been used up to produce something, and hence is not available for use anymore. In economics, a _____ is an alternative that is given up as a result of a decision. In business, the _____ may be one of acquisition, in which case the amount of money expended to acquire it is counted as _____.

- a. Cost
- b. Prime cost
- c. Cost of quality
- d. Cost allocation

4. In financial accounting, _____ or cost of sales includes the direct costs attributable to the production of the goods sold by a company. This amount includes the materials cost used in creating the goods along with the direct labor costs used to produce the good. It excludes indirect expenses such as distribution costs and sales force costs.

- a. Reorder point
- b. 3M Company
- c. FIFO and LIFO accounting
- d. Cost of goods sold

5. _____, Gross profit margin or Gross Profit Rate can be defined as the amount of contribution to the business enterprise, after paying for direct-fixed and direct-variable unit costs, required to cover overheads (fixed commitments) and provide a buffer for unknown items. It expresses the relationship between gross profit and sales revenue.

It can be expressed in absolute terms:

Gross Profit = Revenue − Cost of Goods Sold

or as the ratio of gross profit to sales revenue, usually in the form of a percentage:

_____ Percentage = (Revenue-Cost of Goods Sold)/Revenue

Cost of goods sold includes variable costs and fixed costs directly linked to the product, such as material and labor.

Chapter 4. Reporting and Analyzing Merchandising Operations

a. Gross margin
c. 3M Company
b. BNSF Railway
d. BMC Software, Inc.

6. In accounting, _____ or sales profit is the difference between revenue and the cost of making a product or providing a service, before deducting overhead, payroll, taxation, and interest payments. Note that this is different from operating profit (earnings before interest and taxes.)

Net sales are calculated:

Net sales = Sales - Sales returns and allowances.

a. Participating preferred stock
c. Commercial paper
b. Capital structure
d. Gross profit

7. Discounting is a financial mechanism in which a debtor obtains the right to delay payments to a creditor, for a defined period of time, in exchange for a charge or fee. Essentially, the party that owes money in the present purchases the right to delay the payment until some future date. The _____, or charge, is simply the difference between the original amount owed in the present and the amount that has to be paid in the future to settle the debt.

a. Discount
c. Discount factor
b. Risk aversion
d. Discounting

8. An _____ or bill is a commercial document issued by a seller to the buyer, indicating the products, quantities, and agreed prices for products or services the seller has provided the buyer. An _____ indicates the buyer must pay the seller, according to the payment terms.

In the rental industry, an _____ must include a specific reference to the duration of the time being billed, so rather than quantity, price and discount the invoicing amount is based on quantity, price, discount and duration.

a. ABC Television Network
c. AMEX
b. AIG
d. Invoice

9. _____ refers to a business or organization attempting to acquire goods or services to accomplish the goals of the enterprise. Though there are several organizations that attempt to set standards in the _____ process, processes can vary greatly between organizations. Typically the word e;_____e; is not used interchangeably with the word e;procuremente;, since procurement typically includes Expediting, Supplier Quality, and Traffic and Logistics (T'L) in addition to _____.

a. Supply chain
c. Purchasing
b. Consignor
d. Free port

10. The _____ of 2002 (Pub.L. 107-204, 116 Stat. 745, enacted July 30, 2002), also known as the Public Company Accounting Reform and Investor Protection Act of 2002, is a United States federal law enacted on July 30, 2002 in response to a number of major corporate and accounting scandals including those affecting Enron, Tyco International, Adelphia, Peregrine Systems and WorldCom. The legislation establishes new or enhanced standards for all U.S. public company boards, management, and public accounting firms. It does not apply to privately held companies.

a. Fair Labor Standards Act
b. Lease
c. Sarbanes-Oxley Act
d. FCPA

11. _____ is a file or account that contains money that a person or company owes to suppliers, but has not paid yet (a form of debt.) When you receive an invoice you add it to the file, and then you remove it when you pay. Thus, the A/P is a form of credit that suppliers offer to their purchasers by allowing them to pay for a product or service after it has already been received.

a. Accounts receivable
b. Accrual
c. Earnings before interest, taxes, depreciation and amortization
d. Accounts payable

12. _____ in economics and business is the result of an exchange and from that trade we assign a numerical monetary value to a good, service or asset. If Alice trades Bob 4 apples for an orange, the _____ of an orange is 4 apples. Inversely, the _____ of an apple is 1/4 oranges.

a. Transactional Net Margin Method
b. Discounts and allowances
c. Price discrimination
d. Price

13. _____ are reductions to a basic price of goods or services. They can occur anywhere in the distribution channel, modifying either the manufacturer's list price (determined by the manufacturer and often printed on the package), the retail price (set by the retailer and often attached to the product with a sticker), or the list price (which is quoted to a potential buyer, usually in written form.) The market price (also called effective price) is the amount actually paid.

a. Target costing
b. Resale price maintenance
c. Discounts and allowances
d. Pricing

14. _____ and credit are formal bookkeeping and accounting terms. They are the most fundamental concepts in accounting, representing the two records that one party in a transaction makes on its records, transferring a money balance from one account to another, one representing a reduction of liability or increase in asset, and the other representing a balancing increase in liability or reduction of asset.

Introduction

_____s and credits are a system of notation used in accounting to keep track of money movements (transactions) into and out of an account.

a. Debit
b. Bookkeeping
c. Cookie jar accounting
d. Debit and credit

15. A _____ is the transfer of wealth from one party (such as a person or company) to another. A _____ is usually made in exchange for the provision of goods, services or both, or to fulfill a legal obligation.

The simplest and oldest form of _____ is barter, the exchange of one good or service for another.

a. Payment
b. Payee
c. BMC Software, Inc.
d. 3M Company

Chapter 4. Reporting and Analyzing Merchandising Operations   43

16. Transport or _____ is the movement of people and goods from one location to another. Transport is performed by various modes, such as air, rail, road, water, cable, pipeline and space. The field can be divided into infrastructure, vehicles, and operations.
   a. Transportation
   b. 3M Company
   c. BNSF Railway
   d. BMC Software, Inc.

17. _____ or international commercial terms are a series of international sales terms widely used throughout the world. They are used to divide transaction costs and responsibilities between buyer and seller and reflect state-of-the-art transportation practices. They closely correspond to the U.N. Convention on Contracts for the International Sale of Goods.
   a. AIG
   b. Incoterms
   c. AMEX
   d. ABC Television Network

18. _____ are formal bookkeeping and accounting terms. They are the most fundamental concepts in accounting, representing the two records that one party in a transaction makes on its records, transferring a money balance from one account to another, one representing a reduction of liability or increase in asset, and the other representing a balancing increase in liability or reduction of asset.

   Debits and credits are a system of notation used in accounting to keep track of money movements (transactions) into and out of an account.

   a. Controlling account
   b. Bookkeeping
   c. Debit and credit
   d. Cookie jar accounting

19. An _____ invented by esteemed professor Karen Osterheld is the system of records a business keeps to maintain its accounting system. This includes the purchase, sales, and other financial processes of the business. The purpose of an _____ is to accumulate data and provide decision makers (investors, creditors, and managers) with information to make decision While this was previously a paper-based process, most modern businesses now use accounting software such as UBS, MYOB etc.
   a. ABC Television Network
   b. Accounting information system
   c. AMEX
   d. AIG

20. In accounting/accountancy, _____ are journal entries usually made at the end of an accounting period to allocate income and expenditure to the period in which they actually occurred. The revenue recognition principle is the basis of making _____ that pertain to unearned and accrued revenues under accrual-basis accounting. They are sometimes called Balance Day adjustments because they are made on balance day.
   a. Accrued expense
   b. Accrual
   c. Earnings before interest, taxes, depreciation and amortization
   d. Adjusting entries

21. _____ are journal entries made at the end of an accounting period to transfer temporary accounts to permanent accounts. An 'income summary' account may be used to show the balance between revenue and expenses, or they could be directly closed against retained earnings where dividend payments will be deducted from. This process is used to reset the balance of these temporary accounts to zero for the next accounting period.
   a. Treasury stock
   b. FIFO and LIFO accounting
   c. Closing entries
   d. Trial balance

Chapter 4. Reporting and Analyzing Merchandising Operations

22. Employment is a contract between two parties, one being the employer and the other being the _____. An _____ may be defined as: 'A person in the service of another under any contract of hire, express or implied, oral or written, where the employer has the power or right to control and direct the _____ in the material details of how the work is to be performed.' Black's Law Dictionary page 471 (5th ed. 1979.)

   a. AIG
   b. Employee
   c. AMEX
   d. ABC Television Network

23. _____ is theft of goods from a retail establishment by an ostensible patron. It is one of the most common property crimes dealt with by police and courts.

   Most shoplifters are amateurs; however, there are people and groups who make their living from _____, and they tend to be more skilled.

   a. 3M Company
   b. Shoplifting
   c. BMC Software, Inc.
   d. BNSF Railway

24. In financial accounting the term inventory _____ is the loss of products between point of manufacture or purchase from supplier and point of sale. The term relates to the difference in the amount of margin or profit a retailer can obtain. If the amount of _____ is large, then profits go down which results in increased costs to the consumer to meet the needs of the retailer.

   a. Homogeneous
   b. Shrinkage
   c. Maturity
   d. Screening

25. In business and accounting, _____ are everything of value that is owned by a person or company. It is a claim on the property your income of a borrower. The balance sheet of a firm records the monetary value of the _____ owned by the firm.

   a. Accounts receivable
   b. Assets
   c. Earnings before interest, taxes, depreciation and amortization
   d. Accrual basis accounting

26. _____ are formal records of a business' financial activities.

   In British English, including United Kingdom company law, _____ are often referred to as accounts, although the term _____ is also used, particularly by accountants.

   _____ provide an overview of a business' financial condition in both short and long term.

   a. Statement of retained earnings
   b. Notes to the financial statements
   c. 3M Company
   d. Financial statements

27. _____ are payments made by a corporation to its shareholder members. It is the portion of corporate profits paid out to stockholders. When a corporation earns a profit or surplus, that money can be put to two uses: it can either be re-invested in the business (called retained earnings), or it can be paid to the shareholders as a dividend.

   a. Dividends
   b. Dividend yield
   c. Dividend payout ratio
   d. Dividend stripping

Chapter 4. Reporting and Analyzing Merchandising Operations

28. In accounting, _____ has a very specific meaning. It is an outflow of cash or other valuable assets from a person or company to another person or company. This outflow of cash is generally one side of a trade for products or services that have equal or better current or future value to the buyer than to the seller.
   a. ABC Television Network
   b. AMEX
   c. Expense
   d. AIG

29. _____ is a company's financial statement that indicates how the revenue is transformed into the net income The purpose of the _____ is to show managers and investors whether the company made or lost money during the period being reported.

The important thing to remember about an _____ is that it represents a period of time.

   a. AIG
   b. AMEX
   c. ABC Television Network
   d. Income statement

30. _____ is equal to the income that a firm has after subtracting costs and expenses from the total revenue. _____ can be distributed among holders of common stock as a dividend or held by the firm as retained earnings.

The items deducted will typically include tax expense, financing expense (interest expense), and minority interest. Likewise, preferred stock dividends will be subtracted too, though they are not an expense.

   a. Matching principle
   b. Net income
   c. Long-term liabilities
   d. Generally accepted accounting principles

31. _____, is a liability with an uncertain timing or amount, but where the uncertainty is not significant enough to qualify it as a provision. An example is an unpaid obligation to pay for goods or services received FROM a counterpart, while cash for them is to be paid out in a latter accounting period when its amount is deducted from _____ s.
   a. Accrual basis accounting
   b. Assets
   c. Accounts receivable
   d. Accrued Expense

32. In financial accounting, a _____ or statement of financial position is a summary of a person's or organization's balances. Assets, liabilities and ownership equity are listed as of a specific date, such as the end of its financial year. A _____ is often described as a snapshot of a company's financial condition.
   a. Statement of retained earnings
   b. Financial statements
   c. 3M Company
   d. Balance sheet

33. In finance, the _____ or quick ratio or liquid ratio measures the ability of a company to use its near cash or quick assets to immediately extinguish or retire its current liabilities. Quick assets include those current assets that presumably can be quickly converted to cash at close to their book values.

$$\text{Quick (Acid Test) Ratio} = \frac{\text{Cash} + \text{Marketable Securities} + \text{Accounts Receivables}}{\text{Current Liabilities}}$$

Generally, the acid test ratio should be 1:1 or better, however this varies widely by industry.

a. Invested capital
c. Inventory turnover
b. Earnings per share
d. Acid-test

34. The _____ is a financial ratio that measures whether or not a firm has enough resources to pay its debts over the next 12 months. It compares a firm's current assets to its current liabilities. It is expressed as follows:

$$\text{Current ratio} = \frac{\text{Current Assets}}{\text{Current Liabilities}}$$

For example, if WXY Company's current assets are $50,000,000 and its current liabilities are $40,000,000, then its _____ would be $50,000,000 divided by $40,000,000, which equals 1.25.

a. Current ratio
c. Return on capital
b. Net Interest Income
d. Times interest earned

35. Just in Time could refer to the following:

- _____, an inventory strategy that reduces in-process inventory
- _____ compilation, a technique for improving the performance of bytecode-compiled programming systems

a. Fiscal
c. Help desk and incident reporting auditing
b. Comparable
d. Just-in-time

36. _____ is a business, economics or investment term that refers to an asset's ability to be easily converted through an act of buying or selling without causing a significant movement in the price and with minimum loss of value. Money, or cash on hand, is the most liquid asset. An act of exchange of a less liquid asset with a more liquid asset is called liquidation.

a. Market liquidity
c. Financial instruments
b. Spot rate
d. Transfer agent

37. The _____, a ratio that is typically applied to banks, in simple terms is defined as expenses as a percentage of revenue (expenses / revenue), with a few variations. A lower percentage is better since that means expenses are low and earnings are high. It is related to operating leverage, which measures the ratio between fixed costs and variable costs.

a. Operating leverage
c. Efficiency ratio
b. Equity ratio
d. Average rate of return

38. In business and finance accounting, _____ is equal to the gross profit minus overheads minus interest payable plus/minus one off items for a given time period (usually: accounting period.)

A common synonym for '_____' when discussing financial statements (which include a balance sheet and an income statement) is the bottom line. This term results from the traditional appearance of an income statement which shows all allocated revenues and expenses over a specified time period with the resulting summation on the bottom line of the report.

Chapter 4. Reporting and Analyzing Merchandising Operations

a. Cost of goods sold
c. Salvage value
b. Net profit
d. Treasury stock

39. _____, net margin, net _____ or net profit ratio all refer to a measure of profitability. It is calculated by finding the net profit as a percentage of the revenue.

$$\text{Net profit margin} = \frac{\text{Net profit (after taxes)}}{\text{Revenue}} \times 100$$

The _____ is mostly used for internal comparison.

a. BMC Software, Inc.
c. BNSF Railway
b. 3M Company
d. Profit margin

Chapter 5. Reporting and Analyzing Inventories

1. In a contract of carriage, the _____ is the person to whom the shipment is to be delivered whether by land, sea or air.

This is a difficult area of law in that it regulates the mass transportation industry which cannot always guarantee arrival on time or that goods will not be damaged in the course of transit. A further two problems are that unpaid consignors or freight carriers may wish to hold goods until payment is made, and fraudulent individuals may seek to take delivery in place of the legitimate _____s.

- a. Consignee
- b. Free port
- c. Purchasing
- d. Supply chain

2. The _____, in a contract of carriage, is the person sending a shipment to be delivered whether by land, sea or air. Some carriers, such as national postal entities, use the term 'sender' or 'shipper' but in the event of a legal dispute the proper and technical term '_____' will generally be used.

If Jones sends a widget to Smith via Fred's Delivery Service, Jones is the _____ and Smith is the consignee.

- a. Free port
- b. Purchasing
- c. Consignor
- d. Supply chain

3. _____ is a method of evaluating an asset's worth when held in inventory, in the field of accounting. _____ is part of the Generally Accepted Accounting Principles that apply to valuing inventory, so as to not overstate or understate the value of inventory goods. Net realisable value is generally equal to the selling price of the inventory goods less the selling costs (completion and disposal).
- a. 3M Company
- b. Revenue recognition
- c. BMC Software, Inc.
- d. Net realizable value

4. In economics, business, retail, and accounting, a _____ is the value of money that has been used up to produce something, and hence is not available for use anymore. In economics, a _____ is an alternative that is given up as a result of a decision. In business, the _____ may be one of acquisition, in which case the amount of money expended to acquire it is counted as _____.
- a. Cost
- b. Cost allocation
- c. Cost of quality
- d. Prime cost

5. _____ is the term used to refer to the standard framework of guidelines for financial accounting used in any given jurisdiction. _____ includes the standards, conventions, and rules accountants follow in recording and summarizing transactions, and in the preparation of financial statements.

Financial accounting information must be assembled and reported objectively.

- a. Current asset
- b. Generally accepted accounting principles
- c. General ledger
- d. Long-term liabilities

Chapter 5. Reporting and Analyzing Inventories

6. An _____ is a term used in behavioral economics to describe those types of behaviors that impose costs on a person in the long-run that are not taken into account when making decisions in the present. Classical Economics discourages government from creating legislation that targets internalities, because it is assumed that the consumer takes these personal costs into account when paying for the good that causes the _____. For example, cigarettes should be taxed because of the negative consumption externalities that they impose, such as second-hand smoke, not because the smoker harms him or herself by smoking.
   - a. Inventory turnover ratio
   - b. Operating budget
   - c. Authorised capital
   - d. Internality

7. In accounting and organizational theory, _____ is defined as a process effected by an organization's structure, work and authority flows, people and management information systems, designed to help the organization accomplish specific goals or objectives. It is a means by which an organization's resources are directed, monitored, and measured. It plays an important role in preventing and detecting fraud and protecting the organization's resources, both physical (e.g., machinery and property) and intangible (e.g., reputation or intellectual property such as trademarks.)
   - a. Audit risk
   - b. Internal control
   - c. Auditor independence
   - d. Audit committee

8. _____ is a cornerstone of accrual accounting together with the revenue recognition principle. They both determine the accounting period, in which revenues and expenses are recognized. According to the principle, expenses are recognized when obligations are (1) incurred (usually when goods are transferred or services rendered, e.g. sold), and (2) offset against recognized revenues, which were generated from those expenses (related on the cause-and-effect basis), no matter when cash is paid out.
   - a. Net sales
   - b. Current liabilities
   - c. Payroll
   - d. Matching principle

9. A _____, in business matters, is an entity that is controlled by a bigger and more powerful entity. The controlled entity is called a company, corporation, or limited liability company, and the controlling entity is called its parent (or the parent company.) The reason for this distinction is that a lone company cannot be a _____ of any organization; only an entity representing a legal fiction as a separate entity can be a _____.
   - a. Parent company
   - b. BMC Software, Inc.
   - c. Subsidiary
   - d. 3M Company

10. The _____ is a subset of the general ledger used in accounting. The _____ shows detail for part of the accounting records such as property and equipment, prepaid expenses, etc. The detail would include such items as date the item was purchased or expense incurred, a description of the item, the original balance, and the net book value.
    - a. Subledger
    - b. Credit memo
    - c. Minority interest
    - d. Remittance advice

11. _____ is application software that records and processes accounting transactions within functional modules such as accounts payable, accounts receivable, payroll, and trial balance. It functions as an accounting information system. It may be developed in-house by the company or organization using it, may be purchased from a third party, or may be a combination of a third-party application software package with local modifications.
    - a. Accounting software
    - b. Amgen
    - c. Economic value added
    - d. AIG

12. _____ is a file or account that contains money that a person or company owes to suppliers, but has not paid yet (a form of debt.) When you receive an invoice you add it to the file, and then you remove it when you pay. Thus, the A/P is a form of credit that suppliers offer to their purchasers by allowing them to pay for a product or service after it has already been received.

   a. Accounts receivable
   b. Accrual
   c. Earnings before interest, taxes, depreciation and amortization
   d. Accounts payable

13. Under the average-cost method, it is assumed that the cost of inventory is based on the _____ of the goods available for sale during the period. _____ is computed by dividing the total cost of goods available for sale by the total units available for sale. This gives a weighted-average unit cost that is applied to the units in the ending inventory.

   a. ABC Television Network
   b. AIG
   c. Ending inventory
   d. Average Cost

14. A _____ is the pinnacle activity involved in selling products or services in return for money or other compensation. It is an act of completion of a commercial activity.

   A _____ is completed by the seller, the owner of the goods.

   a. Tertiary sector of economy
   b. Sale
   c. High yield stock
   d. Maturity

15. The _____ of 2002 (Pub.L. 107-204, 116 Stat. 745, enacted July 30, 2002), also known as the Public Company Accounting Reform and Investor Protection Act of 2002, is a United States federal law enacted on July 30, 2002 in response to a number of major corporate and accounting scandals including those affecting Enron, Tyco International, Adelphia, Peregrine Systems and WorldCom. The legislation establishes new or enhanced standards for all U.S. public company boards, management, and public accounting firms. It does not apply to privately held companies.

   a. Fair Labor Standards Act
   b. Lease
   c. FCPA
   d. Sarbanes-Oxley Act

16. A _____ proof is a mathematical proof that a particular theory is consistent. The early development of mathematical proof theory was driven by the desire to provide finitary _____ proofs for all of mathematics as part of Hilbert's program. Hilbert's program was strongly impacted by incompleteness theorems, which showed that sufficiently strong proof theories cannot prove their own _____

   a. Monte Carlo methods
   b. Daybook
   c. Consistency
   d. Consumption

17. _____ methods are means of managing inventory and financial matters involving the money a company ties up within inventory of produced goods, raw materials, parts, components, or feed stocks. FIFO stands for first-in, first-out, meaning that the oldest inventory items are recorded as sold first. LIFO stands for last-in, first-out, meaning that the most recently purchased items are recorded as sold first.

   a. Finished good
   b. Reorder point
   c. 3M Company
   d. FIFO and LIFO accounting

Chapter 5. Reporting and Analyzing Inventories

18. _____ is an approach to valuing and reporting inventory. Normally ending inventory is stated at historical cost (what was paid to obtain it) but there are times when the original cost of the ending inventory is greater than the cost of replacement thus the inventory has lost value. If the inventory has decreased in value below historical cost then its carrying value is reduced and reported on the balance sheet.
 a. Bankruptcy prediction
 b. Lower of cost or market
 c. Remittance advice
 d. Certified Practising Accountant

19. A _____ is any one of a variety of different systems, institutions, procedures, social relations and infrastructures whereby persons trade, and goods and services are exchanged, forming part of the economy. It is an arrangement that allows buyers and sellers to exchange things. _____s vary in size, range, geographic scale, location, types and variety of human communities, as well as the types of goods and services traded.
 a. Perfect competition
 b. Market
 c. Recession
 d. Market Failure

20. _____ is the price at which an asset would trade in a competitive Walrasian auction setting. _____ is often used interchangeably with open _____, fair value or fair _____, although these terms have distinct definitions in different standards, and may differ in some circumstances.

International Valuation Standards defines _____ as 'the estimated amount for which a property should exchange on the date of valuation between a willing buyer and a willing seller in an arme;s-length transaction after proper marketing wherein the parties had each acted knowledgeably, prudently, and without compulsion.'

_____ is a concept distinct from market price, which is e;the price at which one can transacte;, while _____ is e;the true underlying valuee; according to theoretical standards.

 a. Debtor
 b. Market value
 c. Sinking fund
 d. Segregated portfolio company

21. _____ is a political and social term from the Latin verb conservare meaning to save or preserve. As the name suggests it usually indicates support for tradition and traditional values though the meaning has changed in different countries and time periods. The modern political term conservative was used by French politician Chateaubriand in 1819.
 a. Conservatism
 b. Politicized issue
 c. BMC Software, Inc.
 d. 3M Company

22. _____ is a company's financial statement that indicates how the revenue is transformed into the net income The purpose of the _____ is to show managers and investors whether the company made or lost money during the period being reported.

The important thing to remember about an _____ is that it represents a period of time.

 a. AMEX
 b. AIG
 c. ABC Television Network
 d. Income statement

23. In financial accounting, a _____ or statement of financial position is a summary of a person's or organization's balances. Assets, liabilities and ownership equity are listed as of a specific date, such as the end of its financial year. A _____ is often described as a snapshot of a company's financial condition.

a. Statement of retained earnings   b. Financial statements
c. Balance sheet   d. 3M Company

24. _____ is a business, economics or investment term that refers to an asset's ability to be easily converted through an act of buying or selling without causing a significant movement in the price and with minimum loss of value. Money, or cash on hand, is the most liquid asset. An act of exchange of a less liquid asset with a more liquid asset is called liquidation.
  a. Financial instruments   b. Spot rate
  c. Transfer agent   d. Market liquidity

25. The _____, a ratio that is typically applied to banks, in simple terms is defined as expenses as a percentage of revenue (expenses / revenue), with a few variations. A lower percentage is better since that means expenses are low and earnings are high. It is related to operating leverage, which measures the ratio between fixed costs and variable costs.
  a. Average rate of return   b. Equity ratio
  c. Operating leverage   d. Efficiency ratio

26. The _____ is an equation that equals the cost of goods sold divided by the average inventory. Average inventory equals beginning inventory plus ending inventory divided by 2.

The formula for _____:

$$\text{Inventory Turnover} = \frac{\text{Cost of Goods Sold}}{\text{Average Inventory}}$$

The formula for average inventory:

$$\text{Average Inventory} = \frac{\text{Beginning inventory} + \text{Ending inventory}}{2}$$

A low turnover rate may point to overstocking, obsolescence, or deficiencies in the product line or marketing effort.

  a. Enterprise Value/Sales   b. Earnings per share
  c. Upside potential ratio   d. Inventory turnover

27. _____ is one of the Accounting Liquidity ratios, a financial ratio. This ratio measures the number of times, on average, the inventory is sold during the period. Its purpose is to measure the liquidity of the inventory.
  a. ABC Television Network   b. AIG
  c. Ending inventory   d. Inventory turnover Ratio

28. In financial accounting, a _____ is defined as an obligation of an entity arising from past transactions or events, the settlement of which may result in the transfer or use of assets, provision of services or other yielding of economic benefits in the future.

Chapter 5. Reporting and Analyzing Inventories 53

a. Corporate governance
c. False Claims Act
b. Vested
d. Liability

29. _____ consists of the sale of goods or merchandise from a fixed location, such as a department store, boutique or kiosk in small or individual lots for direct consumption by the purchaser. _____ may include subordinated services, such as delivery. Purchasers may be individuals or businesses.

a. BNSF Railway
c. 3M Company
b. BMC Software, Inc.
d. Retailing

30. _____ are formal records of a business' financial activities.

In British English, including United Kingdom company law, _____ are often referred to as accounts, although the term _____ is also used, particularly by accountants.

_____ provide an overview of a business' financial condition in both short and long term.

a. Notes to the financial statements
c. Statement of retained earnings
b. 3M Company
d. Financial statements

31. In accounting, _____ or sales profit is the difference between revenue and the cost of making a product or providing a service, before deducting overhead, payroll, taxation, and interest payments. Note that this is different from operating profit (earnings before interest and taxes.)

Net sales are calculated:

  Net sales = Sales - Sales returns and allowances.

a. Commercial paper
c. Gross profit
b. Participating preferred stock
d. Capital structure

32. _____ is the calculated approximation of a result which is usable even if input data may be incomplete or uncertain.

In statistics, see _____ theory, estimator.

In mathematics, approximation or _____ typically means finding upper or lower bounds of a quantity that cannot readily be computed precisely and is also an educated guess .

a. ABC Television Network
c. Estimation
b. AMEX
d. AIG

Chapter 6. Reporting and Analyzing Cash and Internal Controls

1. An _____ is a term used in behavioral economics to describe those types of behaviors that impose costs on a person in the long-run that are not taken into account when making decisions in the present. Classical Economics discourages government from creating legislation that targets internalities, because it is assumed that the consumer takes these personal costs into account when paying for the good that causes the _____. For example, cigarettes should be taxed because of the negative consumption externalities that they impose, such as second-hand smoke, not because the smoker harms him or herself by smoking.
   a. Operating budget
   b. Authorised capital
   c. Inventory turnover ratio
   d. Internality

2. In accounting and organizational theory, _____ is defined as a process effected by an organization's structure, work and authority flows, people and management information systems, designed to help the organization accomplish specific goals or objectives. It is a means by which an organization's resources are directed, monitored, and measured. It plays an important role in preventing and detecting fraud and protecting the organization's resources, both physical (e.g., machinery and property) and intangible (e.g., reputation or intellectual property such as trademarks.)
   a. Audit risk
   b. Audit committee
   c. Auditor independence
   d. Internal control

3. In business and accounting, _____ are everything of value that is owned by a person or company. It is a claim on the property your income of a borrower. The balance sheet of a firm records the monetary value of the _____ owned by the firm.
   a. Earnings before interest, taxes, depreciation and amortization
   b. Accounts receivable
   c. Accrual basis accounting
   d. Assets

4. Established in 1988 the _____ is the professional organization that governs professional fraud examiners. Its activities include producing fraud information, tools and training. It also governs the professional designation of Certified Fraud Examiner.
   a. AIG
   b. Association of Certified Fraud Examiners
   c. AMEX
   d. ABC Television Network

5. _____ is a designation awarded by the Association of _____s (ACertified Fraud Examiner.) The ACertified Fraud Examiner is a 41,000 member-based global association dedicated to providing anti-fraud education and training.

In order to become a _____ one must meet the following requirements:

- Be an Associate Member of the ACertified Fraud Examiner in good standing
- Meet minimum academic and professional requirements
- Be of high moral character
- Agree to abide by the Bylaws and Code of Professional Ethics of the Association of _____s

Generally, applicants for _____ certification have a minimum of a bachelor's degree or equivalent from an institution of higher education. Two years of professional experience related to fraud can be substituted for each year of college.

   a. Chartered Accountant
   b. Certified Fraud Examiner
   c. Certified public accountant
   d. Chartered Certified Accountant

Chapter 6. Reporting and Analyzing Cash and Internal Controls

6. _____ is the statutory title of qualified accountants in the United States who have passed the Uniform _____ Examination and have met additional state education and experience requirements for certification as a _____. Individuals who have passed the Exam but have not either accomplished the required on-the-job experience or have previously met it but in the meantime have lapsed their continuing professional education are, in many states, permitted the designation '_____ Inactive' or an equivalent phrase. In most U.S. states, only _____s who are licensed are able to provide to the public attestation (including auditing) opinions on financial statements.
- a. Chartered Certified Accountant
- b. Certified General Accountant
- c. Chartered Accountant
- d. Certified public accountant

7. _____ is an agreement, usually secretive, which occurs between two or more persons to deceive, mislead, or defraud others of their legal rights, or to obtain an objective forbidden by law typically involving fraud or gaining an unfair advantage. It is an agreement among firms to divide the market, set prices kickbacks, or misrepresenting the independence of the relationship between the colluding parties.' All acts effected by _____ are considered void.
- a. Debt
- b. Collusion
- c. Limited partnership
- d. Bond market

8. Employment is a contract between two parties, one being the employer and the other being the _____. An _____ may be defined as: 'A person in the service of another under any contract of hire, express or implied, oral or written, where the employer has the power or right to control and direct the _____ in the material details of how the work is to be performed.' Black's Law Dictionary page 471 (5th ed. 1979.)
- a. Employee
- b. AMEX
- c. AIG
- d. ABC Television Network

9. The _____ of 2002 (Pub.L. 107-204, 116 Stat. 745, enacted July 30, 2002), also known as the Public Company Accounting Reform and Investor Protection Act of 2002, is a United States federal law enacted on July 30, 2002 in response to a number of major corporate and accounting scandals including those affecting Enron, Tyco International, Adelphia, Peregrine Systems and WorldCom. The legislation establishes new or enhanced standards for all U.S. public company boards, management, and public accounting firms. It does not apply to privately held companies.
- a. Sarbanes-Oxley Act
- b. FCPA
- c. Fair Labor Standards Act
- d. Lease

10. _____ is the concept of having more than one person required to complete a task. It is alternatively called segregation of duties or, in the political realm, separation of powers.

_____ is one of the key concepts of internal control and is the most difficult and sometimes the most costly one to achieve. The term _____ is already well-known in financial accounting systems. Companies in all sizes understand not to combine roles such as receiving checks (payment on account) and approving write-offs, depositing cash and reconciling bank statements, approving time cards and have custody of pay checks, etc.

- a. 3M Company
- b. Salary
- c. Separation of duties
- d. BMC Software, Inc.

11. An _____ is a practitioner of accountancy, which is the measurement, disclosure or provision of assurance about financial information that helps managers, investors, tax authorities and other decision makers make resource allocation decisions.

The word '_____' is derived from the French 'Compter' which took its origin from the Latin 'Computare'. The word was formerly written in English as 'Accomptant', but in process of time the word, which was always pronounced by dropping the 'p', became gradually changed both in pronunciation and in orthography to its present form.

　a. ABC Television Network　　　　　　　　b. AIG
　c. AMEX　　　　　　　　　　　　　　　　　d. Accountant

12.　_____ is application software that records and processes accounting transactions within functional modules such as accounts payable, accounts receivable, payroll, and trial balance. It functions as an accounting information system. It may be developed in-house by the company or organization using it, may be purchased from a third party, or may be a combination of a third-party application software package with local modifications.
　a. Accounting software　　　　　　　　　　b. Amgen
　c. Economic value added　　　　　　　　　d. AIG

13.　_____ are formal records of a business' financial activities.

In British English, including United Kingdom company law, _____ are often referred to as accounts, although the term _____ is also used, particularly by accountants.

_____ provide an overview of a business' financial condition in both short and long term.

　a. Notes to the financial statements　　　　b. 3M Company
　c. Financial statements　　　　　　　　　　d. Statement of retained earnings

14.　The general definition of an _____ is an evaluation of a person, organization, system, process, project or product. _____s are performed to ascertain the validity and reliability of information; also to provide an assessment of a system's internal control. The goal of an _____ is to express an opinion on the person/organization/system (etc) in question, under evaluation based on work done on a test basis.
　a. Institute of Chartered Accountants of India　　b. Assurance service
　c. Audit regime　　　　　　　　　　　　　　　　　d. Audit

15.　In monetary economics _____ can refer either to a particular _____, for example British Pounds or United States Dollars, or, to the coins and banknotes of a particular _____, which actually form only a small part of the monetary base of a nation's money supply. The other part of a nation's money supply consists of money deposited in banks (sometimes called deposit money), ownership of which can be transferred by means of checks (cheques in the United Kingdom and Australia) or other forms of money transfer such as credit and debit cards. Deposit money and _____ are 'money' in the sense that both are acceptable as a means of exchange, but money need not necessarily be '_____'.
　a. BMC Software, Inc.　　　　　　　　　　b. 3M Company
　c. BNSF Railway　　　　　　　　　　　　　d. Currency

16.　The U.S. _____ is an independent agency of the United States government which holds primary responsibility for enforcing the federal securities laws and regulating the securities industry, the nation's stock and options exchanges, and other electronic securities markets. The SEC was created by section 4 of the Securities Exchange Act of 1934 (now codified as 15 U.S.C. §§ 78d and commonly referred to as the 1934 Act.)

Chapter 6. Reporting and Analyzing Cash and Internal Controls

a. 3M Company
b. BMC Software, Inc.
c. BNSF Railway
d. Securities and Exchange Commission

17. _____ is a term that refers both to:

- a formal discipline used to help appraise, or assess, the case for a project or proposal, which itself is a process known as project appraisal; and
- an informal approach to making decisions of any kind.

Under both definitions the process involves, whether explicitly or implicitly, weighing the total expected costs against the total expected benefits of one or more actions in order to choose the best or most profitable option. The formal process is often referred to as either CBA (_____) or BCost-benefit analysis

A hallmark of CBA is that all benefits and all costs are expressed in money terms, and are adjusted for the time value of money, so that all flows of benefits and flows of project costs over time (which tend to occur at different points in time) are expressed on a common basis in terms of their 'e;present value.'e; Closely related, but slightly different, formal techniques include Cost-effectiveness analysis, Economic impact analysis, Fiscal impact analysis and Social Return on Investment(SROI) analysis. The latter builds upon the logic of _____, but differs in that it is explicitly designed to inform the practical decision-making of enterprise managers and investors focused on optimising their social and environmental impacts.

a. 3M Company
b. Cost-benefit analysis
c. BNSF Railway
d. BMC Software, Inc.

18. A _____, also client, buyer or purchaser is the buyer or user of the paid products of an individual or organization, mostly called the supplier or seller. This is typically through purchasing or renting goods or services.
a. BNSF Railway
b. Customer
c. BMC Software, Inc.
d. 3M Company

19. _____, commonly known as e-commerce or eCommerce, consists of the buying and selling of products or services over electronic systems such as the Internet and other computer networks. The amount of trade conducted electronically has grown extraordinarily since the spread of the Internet. A wide variety of commerce is conducted in this way, spurring and drawing on innovations in electronic funds transfer, supply chain management, Internet marketing, online transaction processing, electronic data interchange (EDI), inventory management systems, and automated data collection systems.
a. Electronic data interchange
b. ABC Television Network
c. AIG
d. Electronic commerce

20. _____ is a specific term used in companies' financial reporting from the company-whole point of view. Because that use excludes the effects of changing ownership interest, an economic measure of _____ is necessary for financial analysis from the shareholders' point of view

_____ is defined by the Financial Accounting Standards Board, or FASB, as 'the change in equity [net assets] of a business enterprise during a period from transactions and other events and circumstances from nonowner sources. It includes all changes in equity during a period except those resulting from investments by owners and distributions to owners.'

_____ is the sum of net income and other items that must bypass the income statement because they have not been realized, including items like an unrealized holding gain or loss from available for sale securities and foreign currency translation gains or losses.

   a. 3M Company   b. BMC Software, Inc.
   c. BNSF Railway   d. Comprehensive income

21. _____ also called 'Internal _____'. It is a term of financial audit, internal audit and Enterprise Risk Management. It means the overall attitude, awareness and actions of directors and management (i.e. 'those charged with governance') regarding the internal control system and its importance to the entity.

   a. Negative assurance   b. Control environment
   c. SOFT audit   d. Mainframe audit

22. A _____ is the transfer of wealth from one party (such as a person or company) to another. A _____ is usually made in exchange for the provision of goods, services or both, or to fulfill a legal obligation.

The simplest and oldest form of _____ is barter, the exchange of one good or service for another.

   a. BMC Software, Inc.   b. Payee
   c. Payment   d. 3M Company

23. _____ is a file or account that contains money that a person or company owes to suppliers, but has not paid yet (a form of debt.) When you receive an invoice you add it to the file, and then you remove it when you pay. Thus, the A/P is a form of credit that suppliers offer to their purchasers by allowing them to pay for a product or service after it has already been received.

   a. Accounts payable   b. Earnings before interest, taxes, depreciation and amortization
   c. Accounts receivable   d. Accrual

24. In accounting, _____ has a very specific meaning. It is an outflow of cash or other valuable assets from a person or company to another person or company. This outflow of cash is generally one side of a trade for products or services that have equal or better current or future value to the buyer than to the seller.

   a. AMEX   b. Expense
   c. ABC Television Network   d. AIG

25. _____ are the most liquid assets found within the asset portion of a company's balance sheet. Cash equivalents are assets that are readily convertible into cash, such as money market holdings, short-term government bonds or Treasury bills, marketable securities and commercial paper. _____ are distinguished from other investments through their short-term existence; they mature within 3 months whereas short-term investments are 12 months or less, and long-term investments are any investments that mature in excess of 12 months.

   a. Payback period   b. Debtor
   c. Par value   d. Cash and cash equivalents

Chapter 6. Reporting and Analyzing Cash and Internal Controls

26. _____ is a business, economics or investment term that refers to an asset's ability to be easily converted through an act of buying or selling without causing a significant movement in the price and with minimum loss of value. Money, or cash on hand, is the most liquid asset. An act of exchange of a less liquid asset with a more liquid asset is called liquidation.
    a. Transfer agent
    b. Market liquidity
    c. Financial instruments
    d. Spot rate

27. In finance, the _____ is the global financial market for short-term borrowing and lending. It provides short-term liquidity funding for the global financial system. The _____ is where short-term obligations such as Treasury bills, commercial paper and bankers' acceptances are bought and sold.
    a. Securitization
    b. Money market
    c. Segregated portfolio company
    d. Restructuring

28. Treasury securities are government debt issued by the United States Department of the Treasury through the Bureau of the Public Debt. They are the debt financing instruments of the U.S. Federal government, and they are often referred to simply as Treasuries or Treasurys. There are four types of marketable treasury securities: _____, Treasury notes, Treasury bonds, and Treasury Inflation Protected Securities (TIPS.)

    _____ mature in one year or less. Like zero-coupon bonds, they do not pay interest prior to maturity; instead they are sold at a discount of the par value to create a positive yield to maturity. Many regard _____ as the least risky investment available to U.S. investors.

    a. BMC Software, Inc.
    b. BNSF Railway
    c. Treasury bills
    d. 3M Company

29. _____ is one of a series of accounting transactions dealing with the billing of customers who owe money to a person, company or organization for goods and services that have been provided to the customer. In most business entities this is typically done by generating an invoice and mailing or electronically delivering it to the customer, who in turn must pay it within an established timeframe called credit or payment terms.

    An example of a common payment term is Net 30, meaning payment is due in the amount of the invoice 30 days from the date of invoice.

    a. Adjusting entries
    b. Accrual
    c. Accounts receivable
    d. Accrued revenue

30. Project _____: The project _____ is a prediction of the costs associated with a particular company project. These costs include labor, materials, and other related expenses. The project _____ is often broken down into specific tasks, with task _____s assigned to each.
    a. BMC Software, Inc.
    b. BNSF Railway
    c. Budget
    d. 3M Company

31. A _____ is any one of a variety of different systems, institutions, procedures, social relations and infrastructures whereby persons trade, and goods and services are exchanged, forming part of the economy. It is an arrangement that allows buyers and sellers to exchange things. _____s vary in size, range, geographic scale, location, types and variety of human communities, as well as the types of goods and services traded.

Chapter 6. Reporting and Analyzing Cash and Internal Controls

a. Market
b. Recession
c. Market Failure
d. Perfect competition

32. _____ is the balance of the amounts of cash being received and paid by a business during a defined period of time, sometimes tied to a specific project. Measurement of _____ can be used

- to evaluate the state or performance of a business or project.
- to determine problems with liquidity. Being profitable does not necessarily mean being liquid. A company can fail because of a shortage of cash, even while profitable.
- to project rate of returns. The time of _____s into and out of projects are used as inputs to financial models such as internal rate of return, and net present value.
- to examine income or growth of a business when it is believed that accrual accounting concepts do not represent economic realities. Alternately, _____ can be used to 'validate' the net income generated by accrual accounting.

_____ as a generic term may be used differently depending on context, and certain _____ definitions may be adapted by analysts and users for their own uses. Common terms include operating _____ and free _____.

a. Commercial paper
b. Flow-through entity
c. Controlling interest
d. Cash flow

33. _____ is often a small amount of discretionary funds in the form of cash used for expenditures where it is not sensible to make the disbursement by check, because of the inconvenience and costs of writing, signing and then cashing the check.

The most common way of accounting expenditures is to use the imprest system. The initial fund would be created by issuing a check for the desired amount.

a. Remittance advice
b. Minority interest
c. Fixed asset
d. Petty cash

34. A _____ is a computer application that simulates a paper worksheet. It displays multiple cells that together make up a grid consisting of rows and columns, each cell containing either alphanumeric text or numeric values. A _____ cell may alternatively contain a formula that defines how the contents of that cell is to be calculated from the contents of any other cell (or combination of cells) each time any cell is updated.

a. Merck ' Co., Inc.
b. Mutual fund
c. Linear regression
d. Spreadsheet

35. In financial accounting, a _____ or Statement of cash flows is a financial statement that shows a company's flow of cash. The money coming into the business is called cash inflow, and money going out from the business is called cash outflow. The statement shows how changes in balance sheet and income accounts affect cash and cash equivalents, and breaks the analysis down to operating, investing, and financing activities.

a. 3M Company
b. BMC Software, Inc.
c. Cash flow statement
d. BNSF Railway

Chapter 6. Reporting and Analyzing Cash and Internal Controls   61

36. A _____ is a bond which is worth a certain monetary value and which may only be spent for specific reasons or on specific goods. Examples include -- but are not limited to -- housing, travel and food _____s. The term _____ is also a synonym for receipt, and is often used to refer to receipts used as evidence of, for example, the declaration that a service has been performed or that an expenditure has been made.
   a. Source document
   b. Voucher
   c. BMC Software, Inc.
   d. 3M Company

37. The _____ is an independent agency of the United States government, established in 1914 by the _____ Act. Its principal mission is the promotion of 'consumer protection' and the elimination and prevention of what regulators perceive to be harmfully 'anti-competitive' business practices, such as coercive monopoly.

The _____ Act was one of President Wilson's major acts against trusts.

   a. BMC Software, Inc.
   b. 3M Company
   c. BNSF Railway
   d. Federal Trade Commission

38. As part of an organization's internal financial controls, the accounting department may institute a _____ process to help manage requests for purchases. Requests for the creation of purchase of goods and services are documented and routed for approval within the organization and then delivered to the accounting group.

Typically an accounting staff member is assigned responsibility for purchase order management, referred to commonly as the PO (purchase order) Coordinator.

   a. BMC Software, Inc.
   b. 3M Company
   c. BNSF Railway
   d. Purchase requisition

39. _____ is a concept that denotes the precise probability of specific eventualities. Technically, the notion of _____ is independent from the notion of value and, as such, eventualities may have both beneficial and adverse consequences. However, in general usage the convention is to focus only on potential negative impact to some characteristic of value that may arise from a future event.
   a. Risk adjusted return on capital
   b. Discount factor
   c. Discounting
   d. Risk

40. The _____ is a form of financial accounting system. The most common _____ is the petty cash system.

The _____ ensures that you must document how the petty cash is spent. In a petty cash system, petty cash dockets are written for each amount issued. So when all of these dockets are totalled at the end of the month and deducted from the opening petty cash float, the calculated value must agree with what is left in the petty cash float. Under the _____, only that which is recorded as spent is replenished.

   a. AMEX
   b. ABC Television Network
   c. AIG
   d. Imprest system

Chapter 6. Reporting and Analyzing Cash and Internal Controls

41. _____ is a fee paid on borrowed assets. It is the price paid for the use of borrowed money, or, money earned by deposited funds. Assets that are sometimes lent with _____ include money, shares, consumer goods through hire purchase, major assets such as aircraft, and even entire factories in finance lease arrangements. The _____ is calculated upon the value of the assets in the same manner as upon money.

   a. ABC Television Network
   b. Insolvency
   c. Interest
   d. AIG

42. An _____ is the price a borrower pays for the use of money they do not own, for instance a small company might borrow from a bank to kick start their business, and the return a lender receives for deferring the use of funds, by lending it to the borrower. _____s are normally expressed as a percentage rate over the period of one year.

   _____s targets are also a vital tool of monetary policy and are used to control variables like investment, inflation, and unemployment.

   a. AMEX
   b. AIG
   c. Interest rate
   d. ABC Television Network

43. In law, the payer is the party making a payment while the _____ is the party receiving the payment.

   There are two types of payment methods; exchanging and provisioning. Exchanging is to change coin, money and banknote in terms of the price.

   a. BMC Software, Inc.
   b. 3M Company
   c. Payee
   d. Payment

44. _____ is the process of matching and comparing figures from accounting records against those presented on a bank statement. Less any items which have no relation to the bank statement, the balance of the accounting ledger should reconcile (match) to the balance of the bank statement.

   _____ allows companies or individuals to compare their account records to the bank's records of their account balance in order to uncover any possible discrepancies.

   a. Lower of Cost or Market
   b. Bankruptcy prediction
   c. Bank reconciliation
   d. Credit memo

45. _____ allows customers to conduct financial transactions on a secure website operated by their retail or virtual bank, credit union or building society.

Chapter 6. Reporting and Analyzing Cash and Internal Controls   63

_____ solutions have many features and capabilities in common, but traditionally also have some that are application specific.

The common features fall broadly into several categories

- Transactional (e.g., performing a financial transaction such as an account to account transfer, paying a bill, wire transfer... and applications... apply for a loan, new account, etc.)
    - Electronic bill presentment and payment - EBPP
    - Funds transfer between a customer's own checking and savings accounts, or to another customer's account
    - Investment purchase or sale
    - Loan applications and transactions, such as repayments

- Non-transactional (e.g., online statements, check links, cobrowsing, chat)
    - Bank statements
- Financial Institution Administration - features allowing the financial institution to manage the online experience of their end users
- ASP/Hosting Administration - features allowing the hosting company to administer the solution across financial institutions

Features commonly unique to business banking include

- Support of multiple users having varying levels of authority
- Transaction approval process
- Wire transfer

Features commonly unique to Internet banking include

- Personal financial management support, such as importing data into personal accounting software. Some _____ platforms support account aggregation to allow the customers to monitor all of their accounts in one place whether they are with their main bank or with other institutions.

a. AMEX
c. AIG
b. ABC Television Network
d. Online banking

46. _____ refers to the computer-based systems used to perform financial transactions electronically.

The term is used for a number of different concepts:

- Cardholder-initiated transactions, where a cardholder makes use of a payment card
- Direct deposit payroll payments for a business to its employees, possibly via a payroll services company
- Direct debit payments from customer to business, where the transaction is initiated by the business with customer permission
- Electronic bill payment in online banking, which may be delivered by _____ or paper check
- Transactions involving stored value of electronic money, possibly in a private currency
- Wire transfer via an international banking network (generally carries a higher fee)
- Electronic Benefit Transfer

electronic funds transferPOS (short for _____ at Point of Sale) is an Australian and New Zealand electronic processing system for credit cards, debit cards and charge cards.

European banks and card companies also sometimes reference 'electronic funds transferPOS' as the system used for processing card transactions through terminals on points of sale, though the system is not the trademarked Australian/New Zealand variant.

Credit cards

_____ may be initiated by a cardholder when a payment card such as a credit card or debit card is used.

a. AIG
b. AMEX
c. Electronic funds transfer
d. ABC Television Network

47. A _____ is a letter sent by a customer to a supplier, to inform the supplier that his invoice has been paid. If the customer is paying by cheque, the _____ often accompanies the cheque.

_____s are not mandatory, but they are seen as a courtesy, because they help the supplier's accounts department to match invoices with payments.

a. Fixed asset
b. Certified Practising Accountant
c. Subledger
d. Remittance advice

48. An account statement or a _____ is a summary of all financial transactions occurring over a given period of time on a deposit account, a credit card, or any other type of account offered by a financial institution.

_____s are typically printed on one or several pieces of paper and either mailed directly to the account holder's address, or kept at the financial institution's local branch for pick-up. Certain ATMs offer the possibility to print, at any time, a condensed version of a _____.

a. BMC Software, Inc.
b. Bank statement
c. 3M Company
d. BNSF Railway

Chapter 6. Reporting and Analyzing Cash and Internal Controls

49. In accounting/accountancy, _____ are journal entries usually made at the end of an accounting period to allocate income and expenditure to the period in which they actually occurred. The revenue recognition principle is the basis of making _____ that pertain to unearned and accrued revenues under accrual-basis accounting. They are sometimes called Balance Day adjustments because they are made on balance day.

a. Adjusting entries
b. Earnings before interest, taxes, depreciation and amortization
c. Accrued expense
d. Accrual

50. An _____ is a computerized telecommunications device that provides the customers of a financial institution with access to financial transactions in a public space without the need for a human clerk or bank teller. On most modern _____s, the customer is identified by inserting a plastic _____ card with a magnetic stripe or a plastic smartcard with a chip, that contains a unique card number and some security information, such as an expiration date or CVC (CVV.) Security is provided by the customer entering a personal identification number (PIN.)

a. Automated teller machine
b. AIG
c. AMEX
d. ABC Television Network

51. In financial accounting and finance, _____ is the portion of receivables that can no longer be collected, typically from accounts receivable or loans. _____ in accounting is considered an expense.

There are two methods to account for _____:

1. Direct write off method (Non - GAAP)

A receivable which is not considered collectible is charged directly to the income statement.

1. Allowance method (GAAP)

An estimate is made at the end of each fiscal year of the amount of _____. This is then accumulated in a provision which is then used to reduce specific receivable accounts as and when necessary.

a. Total Expense Ratio
b. Bad debt
c. 3M Company
d. Tax expense

52. _____ refers to a category of criminal acts that involve making the unlawful use of checks in order to illegally acquire or borrow funds that do not exist within the account balance or account-holder's legal ownership. Most methods involve taking advantage of the float (the time between the negotiation of the cheque and its clearance at the cheque-writer's bank) to draw out these funds. Specific kinds of cheque fraud include cheque kiting, where funds are deposited before the end of the float period to cover the fraud, and paper hanging, where the float offers the opportunity to commit the crime but the account is never replenished.

a. BNSF Railway
b. BMC Software, Inc.
c. Check fraud
d. 3M Company

53. In finance, the _____ between two currencies specifies how much one currency is worth in terms of the other. It is the value of a foreign nation's currency in terms of the home nation's currency. For example an _____ of 102 Japanese yen to the United States dollar means that JPY 102 is worth the same as USD 1.

a. AMEX
b. AIG
c. ABC Television Network
d. Exchange rate

54. '_____' (NSF) is a term used in the banking industry to indicate that a demand for payment (a check) cannot be honored because insufficient funds are available in the account on which the instrument was drawn. In simplified terms, a check has been presented for clearance, but the amount written on the check exceeds the available balance in the account. It is often colloquially referred to as a bad check, a 'bounced' check, or a rubber check.
   a. 3M Company
   b. BMC Software, Inc.
   c. BNSF Railway
   d. Non-sufficient funds

55. _____ is that which is owed; usually referencing assets owed, but the term can also cover moral obligations and other interactions not requiring money. In the case of assets, _____ is a means of using future purchasing power in the present before a summation has been earned. Some companies and corporations use _____ as a part of their overall corporate finance strategy.
   a. Debenture
   b. Debt
   c. Lender
   d. Loan

56. In economics, business, retail, and accounting, a _____ is the value of money that has been used up to produce something, and hence is not available for use anymore. In economics, a _____ is an alternative that is given up as a result of a decision. In business, the _____ may be one of acquisition, in which case the amount of money expended to acquire it is counted as _____.
   a. Cost allocation
   b. Cost of quality
   c. Cost
   d. Prime cost

57. A mutual shareholder or _____ is an individual or company (including a corporation) that legally owns one or more shares of stock in a joint stock company. A company's shareholders collectively own that company. Thus, the typical goal of such companies is to enhance shareholder value.
   a. 3M Company
   b. Growth investing
   c. Stock split
   d. Stockholder

58. The _____, a ratio that is typically applied to banks, in simple terms is defined as expenses as a percentage of revenue (expenses / revenue), with a few variations. A lower percentage is better since that means expenses are low and earnings are high. It is related to operating leverage, which measures the ratio between fixed costs and variable costs.
   a. Average rate of return
   b. Equity ratio
   c. Operating leverage
   d. Efficiency ratio

59. A _____ is the pinnacle activity involved in selling products or services in return for money or other compensation. It is an act of completion of a commercial activity.

A _____ is completed by the seller, the owner of the goods.

   a. Maturity
   b. High yield stock
   c. Tertiary sector of economy
   d. Sale

Chapter 6. Reporting and Analyzing Cash and Internal Controls   67

60. An _____ or bill is a commercial document issued by a seller to the buyer, indicating the products, quantities, and agreed prices for products or services the seller has provided the buyer. An _____ indicates the buyer must pay the seller, according to the payment terms.

In the rental industry, an _____ must include a specific reference to the duration of the time being billed, so rather than quantity, price and discount the invoicing amount is based on quantity, price, discount and duration.

a. ABC Television Network
b. AIG
c. AMEX
d. Invoice

61. A _____ is a commercial document issued by a buyer to a seller, indicating types, quantities, and agreed prices for products or services the seller will provide to the buyer. Sending a _____ to a supplier constitutes a legal offer to buy products or services. Acceptance of a _____ by a seller usually forms a once-off contract between the buyer and seller, so no contract exists until the _____ is accepted.

a. 3M Company
b. BMC Software, Inc.
c. Voucher
d. Purchase order

62. _____ refers to a business or organization attempting to acquire goods or services to accomplish the goals of the enterprise. Though there are several organizations that attempt to set standards in the _____ process, processes can vary greatly between organizations. Typically the word e;_____e; is not used interchangeably with the word e;procuremente;, since procurement typically includes Expediting, Supplier Quality, and Traffic and Logistics (T'L) in addition to _____.

a. Consignor
b. Free port
c. Supply chain
d. Purchasing

63. An _____ invented by esteemed professor Karen Osterheld is the system of records a business keeps to maintain its accounting system. This includes the purchase, sales, and other financial processes of the business. The purpose of an _____ is to accumulate data and provide decision makers (investors, creditors, and managers) with information to make decision While this was previously a paper-based process, most modern businesses now use accounting software such as UBS, MYOB etc.

a. AIG
b. AMEX
c. ABC Television Network
d. Accounting information system

64. A _____ has several related meanings:

- a daily record of events or business; a private _____ is usually referred to as a diary.
- a newspaper or other periodical, in the literal sense of one published each day;
- many publications issued at stated intervals, such as magazines, or scholarly academic _____s, or the record of the transactions of a society, are often called _____s. Although _____ is sometimes used, erroneously, as a synonym for 'magazine,' in academic use, a _____ refers to a serious, scholarly publication, most often peer-reviewed. A non-scholarly magazine written for an educated audience about an industry or an area of professional activity is usually called a professional magazine.

The word 'journalist' for one whose business is writing for the public press has been in use since the end of the 17th century.

Open access _____s are scholarly _____s that are available to the reader without financial or other barrier other than access to the internet itself. Some are subsidized, and some require payment on behalf of the author. Subsidized _____s are financed by an academic institution or a government information center.

   a. BNSF Railway
   c. Journal
   b. 3M Company
   d. BMC Software, Inc.

65. Discounting is a financial mechanism in which a debtor obtains the right to delay payments to a creditor, for a defined period of time, in exchange for a charge or fee. Essentially, the party that owes money in the present purchases the right to delay the payment until some future date. The _____, or charge, is simply the difference between the original amount owed in the present and the amount that has to be paid in the future to settle the debt.
   a. Risk aversion
   c. Discount factor
   b. Discounting
   d. Discount

Chapter 7. Reporting and Analyzing Receivables

1. _____ is one of a series of accounting transactions dealing with the billing of customers who owe money to a person, company or organization for goods and services that have been provided to the customer. In most business entities this is typically done by generating an invoice and mailing or electronically delivering it to the customer, who in turn must pay it within an established timeframe called credit or payment terms.

An example of a common payment term is Net 30, meaning payment is due in the amount of the invoice 30 days from the date of invoice.

    a. Adjusting entries
    b. Accounts receivable
    c. Accrual
    d. Accrued revenue

2. A _____ is the pinnacle activity involved in selling products or services in return for money or other compensation. It is an act of completion of a commercial activity.

A _____ is completed by the seller, the owner of the goods.

    a. Sale
    b. High yield stock
    c. Tertiary sector of economy
    d. Maturity

3. _____ is application software that records and processes accounting transactions within functional modules such as accounts payable, accounts receivable, payroll, and trial balance. It functions as an accounting information system. It may be developed in-house by the company or organization using it, may be purchased from a third party, or may be a combination of a third-party application software package with local modifications.

    a. Economic value added
    b. Amgen
    c. AIG
    d. Accounting software

4. _____ and credit are formal bookkeeping and accounting terms. They are the most fundamental concepts in accounting, representing the two records that one party in a transaction makes on its records, transferring a money balance from one account to another, one representing a reduction of liability or increase in asset, and the other representing a balancing increase in liability or reduction of asset.

Introduction

_____s and credits are a system of notation used in accounting to keep track of money movements (transactions) into and out of an account.

    a. Bookkeeping
    b. Debit and credit
    c. Cookie jar accounting
    d. Debit

5. An _____ is generally a 'disposition of property where at least 1 payment is to be received after the close of the taxable year in which the disposition occurs.'

If a taxpayer realizes income (e.g., gain) from an _____, the income generally must be reported by the taxpayer under the 'installment method.' The 'installment method' is defined as 'a method under which the income recognized for any taxable year [.

a. AMEX
b. Installment sale
c. AIG
d. ABC Television Network

6. In finance, _____ is the process of estimating the potential market value of a financial asset or liability. They can be done on assets (for example, investments in marketable securities such as stocks, options, business enterprises, or intangible assets such as patents and trademarks) or on liabilities (e.g., Bonds issued by a company.) A _____ is required in many contexts including investment analysis, capital budgeting, merger and acquisition transactions, financial reporting, taxable events to determine the proper tax liability, and in litigation.

a. Vyborg Appeal
b. Daybook
c. Disclosure
d. Valuation

7. In financial accounting and finance, _____ is the portion of receivables that can no longer be collected, typically from accounts receivable or loans. _____ in accounting is considered an expense.

There are two methods to account for _____:

1. Direct write off method (Non - GAAP)

A receivable which is not considered collectible is charged directly to the income statement.

1. Allowance method (GAAP)

An estimate is made at the end of each fiscal year of the amount of _____. This is then accumulated in a provision which is then used to reduce specific receivable accounts as and when necessary.

a. Bad debt
b. Tax expense
c. Total Expense Ratio
d. 3M Company

8. _____ is the term used to refer to the standard framework of guidelines for financial accounting used in any given jurisdiction. _____ includes the standards, conventions, and rules accountants follow in recording and summarizing transactions, and in the preparation of financial statements.

Financial accounting information must be assembled and reported objectively.

a. Current asset
b. General ledger
c. Long-term liabilities
d. Generally accepted accounting principles

9. _____ is a cornerstone of accrual accounting together with the revenue recognition principle. They both determine the accounting period, in which revenues and expenses are recognized. According to the principle, expenses are recognized when obligations are (1) incurred (usually when goods are transferred or services rendered, e.g. sold), and (2) offset against recognized revenues, which were generated from those expenses (related on the cause-and-effect basis), no matter when cash is paid out.

a. Payroll
b. Net sales
c. Current liabilities
d. Matching principle

Chapter 7. Reporting and Analyzing Receivables

10. In business and accounting, _____ are everything of value that is owned by a person or company. It is a claim on the property your income of a borrower. The balance sheet of a firm records the monetary value of the _____ owned by the firm.
    a. Accrual basis accounting
    b. Accounts receivable
    c. Assets
    d. Earnings before interest, taxes, depreciation and amortization

11. _____ is that which is owed; usually referencing assets owed, but the term can also cover moral obligations and other interactions not requiring money. In the case of assets, _____ is a means of using future purchasing power in the present before a summation has been earned. Some companies and corporations use _____ as a part of their overall corporate finance strategy.
    a. Lender
    b. Loan
    c. Debenture
    d. Debt

12. The term _____ describes a reduction in recognized value. In accounting terminology, it refers to recognition of the reduced or zero value of an asset. In income tax statements, it refers to a reduction of taxable income as recognition of certain expenses required to produce the income.
    a. Salvage value
    b. Current asset
    c. Payroll
    d. Write-off

13. In monetary economics _____ can refer either to a particular _____, for example British Pounds or United States Dollars, or, to the coins and banknotes of a particular _____, which actually form only a small part of the monetary base of a nation's money supply. The other part of a nation's money supply consists of money deposited in banks (sometimes called deposit money), ownership of which can be transferred by means of checks (cheques in the United Kingdom and Australia) or other forms of money transfer such as credit and debit cards. Deposit money and _____ are 'money' in the sense that both are acceptable as a means of exchange, but money need not necessarily be '_____'.
    a. BMC Software, Inc.
    b. Currency
    c. BNSF Railway
    d. 3M Company

14. In accounting, _____ has a very specific meaning. It is an outflow of cash or other valuable assets from a person or company to another person or company. This outflow of cash is generally one side of a trade for products or services that have equal or better current or future value to the buyer than to the seller.
    a. ABC Television Network
    b. AMEX
    c. Expense
    d. AIG

15. _____ is the calculated approximation of a result which is usable even if input data may be incomplete or uncertain.

In statistics, see _____ theory, estimator.

In mathematics, approximation or _____ typically means finding upper or lower bounds of a quantity that cannot readily be computed precisely and is also an educated guess .

    a. AIG
    b. AMEX
    c. Estimation
    d. ABC Television Network

Chapter 7. Reporting and Analyzing Receivables

16. _____ is a fee paid on borrowed assets. It is the price paid for the use of borrowed money, or, money earned by deposited funds. Assets that are sometimes lent with _____ include money, shares, consumer goods through hire purchase, major assets such as aircraft, and even entire factories in finance lease arrangements. The _____ is calculated upon the value of the assets in the same manner as upon money.

   a. ABC Television Network   b. AIG
   c. Insolvency   d. Interest

17. _____ is a life of security. It may also refer to the final payment date of a loan or other financial instrument, at which point all remaining interest and principal is due to be paid.

1, 3, 6 months _____ band can be calculated by using 30-day per month periods. For _____ bands over a year it is acceptable to use 365 day per year. For example with a Treasury Bond, its _____ is the date on which the principal is paid.

   a. Factor   b. The Goodyear Tire ' Rubber Company
                                                         d. Statements of Financial Accounting Standards No.
   c. Maturity   133, Accounting for Derivative Instruments and Hedging
                                                         Activities

18. A _____, also referred to as a note payable in accounting, is a contract where one party (the maker or issuer) makes an unconditional promise in writing to pay a sum of money to the other (the payee), either at a fixed or determinable future time or on demand of the payee, under specific terms. They differ from IOUs in that they contain a specific promise to pay, rather than simply acknowledging that a debt exists.

The terms of a note typically include the principal amount, the interest rate if any, and the maturity date.

   a. BMC Software, Inc.   b. Promissory note
   c. 3M Company   d. BNSF Railway

19. _____ represents claims for which formal instruments of credit are issued as evidence of debt, such as a promissory note. The credit instrument normally requires the debtor to pay interest and extends for time periods of 60-90 days or longer.

   a. Restricted stock   b. Public offering
   c. Notes receivable   d. Moving average

20. In law, the payer is the party making a payment while the _____ is the party receiving the payment.

There are two types of payment methods; exchanging and provisioning. Exchanging is to change coin, money and banknote in terms of the price.

   a. Payment   b. BMC Software, Inc.
   c. 3M Company   d. Payee

21. In accounting, _____ or carrying value is the value of an asset according to its balance sheet account balance. For assets, the value is based on the original cost of the asset less any depreciation, amortization or impairment costs made against the asset. Traditionally, a company's _____ is its total assets minus intangible assets and liabilities.

Chapter 7. Reporting and Analyzing Receivables

a. Generally accepted accounting principles
b. Book value
c. Matching principle
d. Depreciation

22. In financial accounting, a _____ is defined as an obligation of an entity arising from past transactions or events, the settlement of which may result in the transfer or use of assets, provision of services or other yielding of economic benefits in the future.
   a. False Claims Act
   b. Corporate governance
   c. Vested
   d. Liability

23. A _____, in business matters, is an entity that is controlled by a bigger and more powerful entity. The controlled entity is called a company, corporation, or limited liability company, and the controlling entity is called its parent (or the parent company.) The reason for this distinction is that a lone company cannot be a _____ of any organization; only an entity representing a legal fiction as a separate entity can be a _____.
   a. Parent company
   b. BMC Software, Inc.
   c. 3M Company
   d. Subsidiary

24. The _____ is a subset of the general ledger used in accounting. The _____ shows detail for part of the accounting records such as property and equipment, prepaid expenses, etc. The detail would include such items as date the item was purchased or expense incurred, a description of the item, the original balance, and the net book value.
   a. Credit memo
   b. Subledger
   c. Remittance advice
   d. Minority interest

25. _____ is a file or account that contains money that a person or company owes to suppliers, but has not paid yet (a form of debt.) When you receive an invoice you add it to the file, and then you remove it when you pay. Thus, the A/P is a form of credit that suppliers offer to their purchasers by allowing them to pay for a product or service after it has already been received.
   a. Earnings before interest, taxes, depreciation and amortization
   b. Accrual
   c. Accounts payable
   d. Accounts receivable

26. An _____ is a period with reference to which United Kingdom corporation tax is charged. It helps dictate when tax is paid on income and gains. An _____ begins whenever a company comes within the corporation tax charge, and whenever an _____ ends without the company ceasing to be within the charge.
   a. AMEX
   b. Accounting period
   c. ABC Television Network
   d. AIG

27. In accounting/accountancy, _____ are journal entries usually made at the end of an accounting period to allocate income and expenditure to the period in which they actually occurred. The revenue recognition principle is the basis of making _____ that pertain to unearned and accrued revenues under accrual-basis accounting. They are sometimes called Balance Day adjustments because they are made on balance day.
   a. Accrued expense
   b. Accrual
   c. Earnings before interest, taxes, depreciation and amortization
   d. Adjusting entries

Chapter 7. Reporting and Analyzing Receivables

28. _____ is the process of matching and comparing figures from accounting records against those presented on a bank statement. Less any items which have no relation to the bank statement, the balance of the accounting ledger should reconcile (match) to the balance of the bank statement.

_____ allows companies or individuals to compare their account records to the bank's records of their account balance in order to uncover any possible discrepancies.

a. Bankruptcy prediction	b. Credit memo
c. Lower of Cost or Market	d. Bank reconciliation

29. In mathematics _____s are numbers or other things that get multiplied. In particular, see:

- Factorization, the decomposition of an object into a product of other objects
- Integer factorization, the process of breaking down a composite number into smaller non-trivial divisors
- A coefficient
- A divisor of a particular number, or of an element of a monoid
- A von Neumann algebra with a trivial center

In statistics

- _____ analysis is the study of how _____s or certain variables affect variables.

In technology:

- Human _____s, a profession that focuses on how people interact with products, tools, or procedures
- 'Functionality, Application domain, Conditions, Technology, Objects and Responsibility;', In object-oriented programming

In computer science and information technology:

- Authentication _____, a piece of information used to verify a person's identity for security purposes
- _____, a Unix command for numbers factorization
- _____ (programming language), an experimental Forth-like programming language

In television:

- The O'Reilly _____, an American talk show hosted by Bill O'Reilly on Fox News.
- The Krypton _____, a British game show hosted by Gordon Burns, formally on ITV. Also had an American version.

a. Merck ' Co., Inc.	b. The Goodyear Tire ' Rubber Company
c. Factor	d. Valuation

Chapter 7. Reporting and Analyzing Receivables

30. _____ is the risk of loss due to a debtor's non-payment of a loan or other line of credit (either the principal or interest (coupon) or both)

Most lenders employ their own models (credit scorecards) to rank potential and existing customers according to risk, and then apply appropriate strategies. With products such as unsecured personal loans or mortgages, lenders charge a higher price for higher risk customers and vice versa. With revolving products such as credit cards and overdrafts, risk is controlled through the setting of credit limits.

a. 3M Company
c. Market risk
b. Currency risk
d. Credit risk

31. _____ is a business, economics or investment term that refers to an asset's ability to be easily converted through an act of buying or selling without causing a significant movement in the price and with minimum loss of value. Money, or cash on hand, is the most liquid asset. An act of exchange of a less liquid asset with a more liquid asset is called liquidation.

a. Transfer agent
c. Financial instruments
b. Spot rate
d. Market liquidity

32. The _____ of 2002 (Pub.L. 107-204, 116 Stat. 745, enacted July 30, 2002), also known as the Public Company Accounting Reform and Investor Protection Act of 2002, is a United States federal law enacted on July 30, 2002 in response to a number of major corporate and accounting scandals including those affecting Enron, Tyco International, Adelphia, Peregrine Systems and WorldCom. The legislation establishes new or enhanced standards for all U.S. public company boards, management, and public accounting firms. It does not apply to privately held companies.

a. Lease
c. FCPA
b. Sarbanes-Oxley Act
d. Fair Labor Standards Act

33. A _____ is a bond which is worth a certain monetary value and which may only be spent for specific reasons or on specific goods. Examples include -- but are not limited to -- housing, travel and food _____s. The term _____ is also a synonym for receipt, and is often used to refer to receipts used as evidence of, for example, the declaration that a service has been performed or that an expenditure has been made.

a. Source document
c. 3M Company
b. BMC Software, Inc.
d. Voucher

34. The _____, a ratio that is typically applied to banks, in simple terms is defined as expenses as a percentage of revenue (expenses / revenue), with a few variations. A lower percentage is better since that means expenses are low and earnings are high. It is related to operating leverage, which measures the ratio between fixed costs and variable costs.

a. Equity ratio
c. Efficiency ratio
b. Operating leverage
d. Average rate of return

35. A _____ is a type of debt Like all debt instruments, a _____ entails the redistribution of financial assets over time, between the lender and the borrower.

a. Debenture
c. Loan to value
b. Lender
d. Loan

36. _____ is one of the accounting liquidity ratios, a financial ratio. This ratio measures the number of times, on average, receivables (e.g. Accounts Receivable) are collected during the period. A popular variant of the _____ is to convert it into an Average Collection Period in terms of days.

a. Receivable turnover Ratio	b. Shrinkage
c. Capital	d. Price-to-sales ratio

37. _____ is a concept that denotes the precise probability of specific eventualities. Technically, the notion of _____ is independent from the notion of value and, as such, eventualities may have both beneficial and adverse consequences. However, in general usage the convention is to focus only on potential negative impact to some characteristic of value that may arise from a future event.

a. Risk	b. Risk adjusted return on capital
c. Discounting	d. Discount factor

Chapter 8. Reporting and Analyzing Long-Term Assets

1. In business and accounting, _____ are everything of value that is owned by a person or company. It is a claim on the property your income of a borrower. The balance sheet of a firm records the monetary value of the _____ owned by the firm.
   a. Earnings before interest, taxes, depreciation and amortization
   b. Accrual basis accounting
   c. Accounts receivable
   d. Assets

2. In economics, _____ or _____ goods or real _____ refers to factors of production used to create goods or services that are not themselves significantly consumed (though they may depreciate) in the production process. _____ goods may be acquired with money or financial _____. In finance and accounting, _____ generally refers to financial wealth, especially that used to start or maintain a business.
   a. Disclosure
   b. Screening
   c. Vyborg Appeal
   d. Capital

3. A _____ is an expenditure creating future benefits. A _____ is incurred when a business spends money either to buy fixed assets or to add to the value of an existing fixed asset with a useful life that extends beyond the taxable year. Capex are used by a company to acquire or upgrade physical assets such as equipment, property, or industrial buildings.
   a. Cost of capital
   b. Capital expenditure
   c. 3M Company
   d. BMC Software, Inc.

4. _____ is a specific term used in companies' financial reporting from the company-whole point of view. Because that use excludes the effects of changing ownership interest, an economic measure of _____ is necessary for financial analysis from the shareholders' point of view

   _____ is defined by the Financial Accounting Standards Board, or FASB, as 'the change in equity [net assets] of a business enterprise during a period from transactions and other events and circumstances from nonowner sources. It includes all changes in equity during a period except those resulting from investments by owners and distributions to owners.'

   _____ is the sum of net income and other items that must bypass the income statement because they have not been realized, including items like an unrealized holding gain or loss from available for sale securities and foreign currency translation gains or losses.

   a. 3M Company
   b. BNSF Railway
   c. BMC Software, Inc.
   d. Comprehensive income

Chapter 8. Reporting and Analyzing Long-Term Assets

5. _____ is the balance of the amounts of cash being received and paid by a business during a defined period of time, sometimes tied to a specific project. Measurement of _____ can be used

- to evaluate the state or performance of a business or project.
- to determine problems with liquidity. Being profitable does not necessarily mean being liquid. A company can fail because of a shortage of cash, even while profitable.
- to project rate of returns. The time of _____s into and out of projects are used as inputs to financial models such as internal rate of return, and net present value.
- to examine income or growth of a business when it is believed that accrual accounting concepts do not represent economic realities. Alternately, _____ can be used to 'validate' the net income generated by accrual accounting.

_____ as a generic term may be used differently depending on context, and certain _____ definitions may be adapted by analysts and users for their own uses. Common terms include operating _____ and free _____.

- a. Cash flow
- b. Commercial paper
- c. Controlling interest
- d. Flow-through entity

6. In financial accounting, a _____ or statement of financial position is a summary of a person's or organization's balances. Assets, liabilities and ownership equity are listed as of a specific date, such as the end of its financial year. A _____ is often described as a snapshot of a company's financial condition.
- a. Financial statements
- b. Balance sheet
- c. 3M Company
- d. Statement of retained earnings

7. In economics, business, retail, and accounting, a _____ is the value of money that has been used up to produce something, and hence is not available for use anymore. In economics, a _____ is an alternative that is given up as a result of a decision. In business, the _____ may be one of acquisition, in which case the amount of money expended to acquire it is counted as _____.
- a. Prime cost
- b. Cost allocation
- c. Cost
- d. Cost of quality

8. _____ was a maxim coined by Josiah Warren, indicating a (prescriptive) version of the labor theory of value. Warren maintained that the just compensation for labor (or for its product) could only be an equivalent amount of labor (or a product embodying an equivalent amount.) Thus, profit, rent, and interest were considered unjust economic arrangements.
- a. Politicized issue
- b. BMC Software, Inc.
- c. 3M Company
- d. Cost the limit of price

9. _____ is a company's financial statement that indicates how the revenue is transformed into the net income The purpose of the _____ is to show managers and investors whether the company made or lost money during the period being reported.

The important thing to remember about an _____ is that it represents a period of time.

- a. AIG
- b. ABC Television Network
- c. AMEX
- d. Income statement

Chapter 8. Reporting and Analyzing Long-Term Assets

10. In finance, _____ is the process of estimating the potential market value of a financial asset or liability. They can be done on assets (for example, investments in marketable securities such as stocks, options, business enterprises, or intangible assets such as patents and trademarks) or on liabilities (e.g., Bonds issued by a company.) A _____ is required in many contexts including investment analysis, capital budgeting, merger and acquisition transactions, financial reporting, taxable events to determine the proper tax liability, and in litigation.
    a. Vyborg Appeal
    b. Valuation
    c. Daybook
    d. Disclosure

11. _____ or land amelioration refers to investments making land more usable by humans. In terms of accounting, _____s refer to any variety of projects that increase the value of the property. Most are depreciable, but some _____s are not able to be depreciated because a useful life cannot be determined.
    a. BNSF Railway
    b. 3M Company
    c. BMC Software, Inc.
    d. Land improvement

12. A _____ is a one-time payment of money, as opposed to a series of payments made over time.
    a. Trade name
    b. Redemption value
    c. Manufacturing operations
    d. Lump sum

13. A _____ is any one of a variety of different systems, institutions, procedures, social relations and infrastructures whereby persons trade, and goods and services are exchanged, forming part of the economy. It is an arrangement that allows buyers and sellers to exchange things. _____s vary in size, range, geographic scale, location, types and variety of human communities, as well as the types of goods and services traded.
    a. Recession
    b. Market
    c. Market Failure
    d. Perfect competition

14. _____ is the price at which an asset would trade in a competitive Walrasian auction setting. _____ is often used interchangeably with open _____, fair value or fair _____, although these terms have distinct definitions in different standards, and may differ in some circumstances.

    International Valuation Standards defines _____ as 'the estimated amount for which a property should exchange on the date of valuation between a willing buyer and a willing seller in an arme;s-length transaction after proper marketing wherein the parties had each acted knowledgeably, prudently, and without compulsion.'

    _____ is a concept distinct from market price, which is e;the price at which one can transacte;, while _____ is e;the true underlying valuee; according to theoretical standards.

    a. Market value
    b. Debtor
    c. Sinking fund
    d. Segregated portfolio company

15. _____ refers to a business or organization attempting to acquire goods or services to accomplish the goals of the enterprise. Though there are several organizations that attempt to set standards in the _____ process, processes can vary greatly between organizations. Typically the word e;_____e; is not used interchangeably with the word e;procuremente;, since procurement typically includes Expediting, Supplier Quality, and Traffic and Logistics (T'L) in addition to _____.

Chapter 8. Reporting and Analyzing Long-Term Assets

a. Free port
b. Consignor
c. Supply chain
d. Purchasing

16. _____ represents claims for which formal instruments of credit are issued as evidence of debt, such as a promissory note. The credit instrument normally requires the debtor to pay interest and extends for time periods of 60-90 days or longer.

a. Public offering
b. Restricted stock
c. Moving average
d. Notes receivable

17. _____ is a term used in accounting, economics and finance to spread the cost of an asset over the span of several years.

In simple words we can say that _____ is the reduction in the value of an asset due to usage, passage of time, wear and tear, technological outdating or obsolescence, depletion, inadequacy, rot, rust, decay or other such factors.

In accounting, _____ is a term used to describe any method of attributing the historical or purchase cost of an asset across its useful life, roughly corresponding to normal wear and tear.

a. General ledger
b. Current asset
c. Net profit
d. Depreciation

18. Straight-line depreciation is the simplest and most often used technique, in which the company estimates the _____ of the asset at the end of the period during which it will be used to generate revenues (useful life), and will expense a portion of original cost in equal increments over that period. The _____ is an estimate of the value of the asset at the time it will be sold or disposed of; it may be zero. _____ is scrap value, by another name.

a. Net profit
b. Closing entries
c. Generally accepted accounting principles
d. Salvage value

19. In mathematics _____s are numbers or other things that get multiplied. In particular, see:

- Factorization, the decomposition of an object into a product of other objects
- Integer factorization, the process of breaking down a composite number into smaller non-trivial divisors
- A coefficient
- A divisor of a particular number, or of an element of a monoid
- A von Neumann algebra with a trivial center

In statistics

- _____ analysis is the study of how _____s or certain variables affect variables.

Chapter 8. Reporting and Analyzing Long-Term Assets

In technology:

- Human _____s, a profession that focuses on how people interact with products, tools, or procedures
- 'Functionality, Application domain, Conditions, Technology, Objects and Responsibility;', In object-oriented programming

In computer science and information technology:

- Authentication _____, a piece of information used to verify a person's identity for security purposes
- _____, a Unix command for numbers factorization
- _____ (programming language), an experimental Forth-like programming language

In television:

- The O'Reilly _____, an American talk show hosted by Bill O'Reilly on Fox News.
- The Krypton _____, a British game show hosted by Gordon Burns, formally on ITV. Also had an American version.

.

a. The Goodyear Tire ' Rubber Company
c. Valuation
b. Merck ' Co., Inc.
d. Factor

20. _____ is an acronym for First In, First Out, an abstraction in ways of organizing and manipulation of data relative to time and prioritization. This expression describes the principle of a queue processing technique or servicing conflicting demands by ordering process by first-come, first-served (FCFS) behaviour: what comes in first is handled first, what comes in next waits until the first is finished, etc.

Thus it is analogous to the behaviour of persons queueing (or 'standing in line', in common American parlance), where the persons leave the queue in the order they arrive, or waiting one's turn at a traffic control signal.

a. Trademark
c. Kanban
b. Risk management
d. FIFO

21. There are several methods for calculating depreciation, generally based on either the passage of time or the level of activity (or use) of the asset.

_____ is the simplest and most often used technique, in which the company estimates the salvage value of the asset at the end of the period during which it will be used to generate revenues (useful life), and will expense a portion of original cost in equal increments over that period.

a. Closing entries
c. Pro forma
b. Current asset
d. Straight-line depreciation

Chapter 8. Reporting and Analyzing Long-Term Assets

22. In accounting, _____ or carrying value is the value of an asset according to its balance sheet account balance. For assets, the value is based on the original cost of the asset less any depreciation, amortization or impairment costs made against the asset. Traditionally, a company's _____ is its total assets minus intangible assets and liabilities.
    - a. Depreciation
    - b. Matching principle
    - c. Generally accepted accounting principles
    - d. Book value

23. In physics, and more specifically kinematics, _____ is the change in velocity over time. Because velocity is a vector, it can change in two ways: a change in magnitude and/or a change in direction. In one dimension, _____ is the rate at which something speeds up or slows down.
    - a. ABC Television Network
    - b. Acceleration
    - c. AIG
    - d. AMEX

24. _____ refers to any one of several methods by which a company, for 'financial accounting' and/or tax purposes, depreciates a fixed asset in such a way that the amount of depreciation taken each year is higher during the earlier years of an assete;s life. For financial accounting purposes, _____ is generally used when an asset is expected to be much more productive during its early years, so that depreciation expense will more accurately represent how much of an assete;s usefulness is being used up each year. For tax purposes, _____ provides a way of deferring corporate income taxes by reducing taxable income in current years, in exchange for increased taxable income in future years.
    - a. Indirect tax
    - b. User charge
    - c. Effective marginal tax rates
    - d. Accelerated depreciation

25. The _____ is the current method of accelerated asset depreciation required by the United States income tax code. Under _____, all assets are divided into classes which dictate the number of years over which an asset's cost will be recovered.

    Prior to the Accelerated Cost Recovery System (ACRS), most capital purchases were depreciated using a straight line technique, that allowed for the depreciation of the asset over its useful life.

    - a. BMC Software, Inc.
    - b. 3M Company
    - c. Categorical grants
    - d. Modified Accelerated Cost Recovery System

26. _____ is application software that records and processes accounting transactions within functional modules such as accounts payable, accounts receivable, payroll, and trial balance. It functions as an accounting information system. It may be developed in-house by the company or organization using it, may be purchased from a third party, or may be a combination of a third-party application software package with local modifications.
    - a. AIG
    - b. Economic value added
    - c. Accounting software
    - d. Amgen

27. The _____ is a United States federal law that imposes a federal employer tax used to fund state workforce agencies. Employers report this tax by filing an annual Form 940 with the Internal Revenue Service.
    - a. Federal Unemployment Tax Act
    - b. Council Tax
    - c. Transfer tax
    - d. Tax evasion

Chapter 8. Reporting and Analyzing Long-Term Assets

28. A _____, in business matters, is an entity that is controlled by a bigger and more powerful entity. The controlled entity is called a company, corporation, or limited liability company, and the controlling entity is called its parent (or the parent company.) The reason for this distinction is that a lone company cannot be a _____ of any organization; only an entity representing a legal fiction as a separate entity can be a _____.

   a. Subsidiary
   b. Parent company
   c. BMC Software, Inc.
   d. 3M Company

29. The _____ is a subset of the general ledger used in accounting. The _____ shows detail for part of the accounting records such as property and equipment, prepaid expenses, etc. The detail would include such items as date the item was purchased or expense incurred, a description of the item, the original balance, and the net book value.

   a. Remittance advice
   b. Minority interest
   c. Credit memo
   d. Subledger

30. An _____ is a period with reference to which United Kingdom corporation tax is charged. It helps dictate when tax is paid on income and gains. An _____ begins whenever a company comes within the corporation tax charge, and whenever an _____ ends without the company ceasing to be within the charge.

   a. AMEX
   b. Accounting period
   c. ABC Television Network
   d. AIG

31. _____ is a file or account that contains money that a person or company owes to suppliers, but has not paid yet (a form of debt.) When you receive an invoice you add it to the file, and then you remove it when you pay. Thus, the A/P is a form of credit that suppliers offer to their purchasers by allowing them to pay for a product or service after it has already been received.

   a. Accounts receivable
   b. Accounts payable
   c. Accrual
   d. Earnings before interest, taxes, depreciation and amortization

32. _____ are formal bookkeeping and accounting terms. They are the most fundamental concepts in accounting, representing the two records that one party in a transaction makes on its records, transferring a money balance from one account to another, one representing a reduction of liability or increase in asset, and the other representing a balancing increase in liability or reduction of asset.

Debits and credits are a system of notation used in accounting to keep track of money movements (transactions) into and out of an account.

   a. Debit and credit
   b. Bookkeeping
   c. Controlling account
   d. Cookie jar accounting

33. _____ is the term used to refer to the standard framework of guidelines for financial accounting used in any given jurisdiction. _____ includes the standards, conventions, and rules accountants follow in recording and summarizing transactions, and in the preparation of financial statements.

Financial accounting information must be assembled and reported objectively.

Chapter 8. Reporting and Analyzing Long-Term Assets

a. General ledger
b. Long-term liabilities
c. Current asset
d. Generally accepted accounting principles

34. An _____, operating expenditure, operational expense, operational expenditure or OPEX is an on-going cost for running a product, business, or system. Its counterpart, a capital expenditure (CAPEX), is the cost of developing or providing non-consumable parts for the product or system. For example, the purchase of a photocopier is the CAPEX, and the annual paper and toner cost is the OPEX.
  a. AMEX
  b. AIG
  c. ABC Television Network
  d. Operating expense

35. _____, making better, is a general term used particularly in connection with the increased value given to real property by causes for which a tenant or the public, but not the owner, is responsible; it is thus of the nature of unearned increment. When, for instance, some public improvement results in raising the value of a piece of private land, and the owner is thereby bettered through no merit of his own, he gains by the _____, and many economists and politicians have sought to arrange, by taxation or otherwise, that the increased value shall come into the pocket of the public rather than into the owner's. A _____ tax would be so assessed as to divert from the owner of the property the profit thus accruing unearned to him.
  a. Fiduciary
  b. Betterment
  c. Malpractice
  d. Secondary authority

36. _____ is a cornerstone of accrual accounting together with the revenue recognition principle. They both determine the accounting period, in which revenues and expenses are recognized. According to the principle, expenses are recognized when obligations are (1) incurred (usually when goods are transferred or services rendered, e.g. sold), and (2) offset against recognized revenues, which were generated from those expenses (related on the cause-and-effect basis), no matter when cash is paid out.
  a. Matching principle
  b. Payroll
  c. Current liabilities
  d. Net sales

37. _____ is fixing any sort of mechanical or electrical device should it become out of order or broken (known as repair or unscheduled maintenance) as well as performing the routine actions which keep the device in working order (known as scheduled maintenance) or prevent trouble from arising (preventive maintenance.) The MRO business is seeing a major boom with the emergence of international carriers and private aviation in Asia. The MRO business in India alone is expected to grow to $45Bn from the current $0.5Bn in the next decade.
  a. 3M Company
  b. BMC Software, Inc.
  c. BNSF Railway
  d. Maintenance, repair and operations

38. A _____ is the pinnacle activity involved in selling products or services in return for money or other compensation. It is an act of completion of a commercial activity.

A _____ is completed by the seller, the owner of the goods.

  a. Sale
  b. High yield stock
  c. Maturity
  d. Tertiary sector of economy

39. The Exxon Mobil Corporation is an American oil and gas corporation. It is a direct descendant of John D. Rockefeller's Standard Oil company, formed on November 30, 1999, by the merger of Exxon and Mobil.

Chapter 8. Reporting and Analyzing Long-Term Assets 85

_____ is the world's largest publicly traded company when measured by either revenue or market capitalization.

a. Abby Joseph Cohen
c. Arthur Betz Laffer
b. Alan Greenspan
d. ExxonMobil

40. In economic models, the _____ time frame assumes no fixed factors of production. Firms can enter or leave the marketplace, and the cost (and availability) of land, labor, raw materials, and capital goods can be assumed to vary. In contrast, in the short-run time frame, certain factors are assumed to be fixed, because there is not sufficient time for them to change.

a. Short-run
c. BMC Software, Inc.
b. Long-run
d. 3M Company

41. _____ is the process of increasing, or accounting for, an amount over a period of time. Particular instances of the term include:

- _____, the allocation of a lump sum amount to different time periods, particularly for loans and other forms of finance, including related interest or other finance charges.
    - _____ schedule, a table detailing each periodic payment on a loan (typically a mortgage), as generated by an _____ calculator.
    - Negative _____, an _____ schedule where the loan amount actually increases through not paying the full interest
- Amortized analysis, analyzing the execution cost of algorithms over a sequence of operations.
- _____ of capital expenditures of certain assets under accounting rules, particularly intangible assets, in a manner analogous to depreciation.
- _____

a. Annuity
c. Intangible
b. Amortization
d. EBIT

42. _____ are defined as identifiable non-monetary assets that cannot be seen, touched or physically measured, which are created through time and/or effort and that are identifiable as a separate asset. There are two primary forms of intangibles - legal intangibles (such as trade secrets (e.g., customer lists), copyrights, patents, trademarks, and goodwill) and competitive intangibles (such as knowledge activities (know-how, knowledge), collaboration activities, leverage activities, and structural activities.) Legal intangibles are known under the generic term intellectual property and generate legal property rights defensible in a court of law.

a. Overhead
c. AIG
b. ABC Television Network
d. Intangible assets

43. _____ is a type of lease - the other being an operating lease. A _____ effectively allows a firm to finance the purchase of an asset, even if, strictly speaking, the firm never acquires the asset. Typically, a _____ will give the lessee control over an asset for a large proportion of the asset's useful life, providing them the benefits and risks of ownership.

a. Debt ratio
c. Finance lease
b. 3M Company
d. Profitability index

Chapter 8. Reporting and Analyzing Long-Term Assets

44. A _____ is a contract conferring a right on one person to possess property belonging to another person (called a landlord or lessor) to the exclusion of the owner landlord. It is a rental agreement between landlord and tenant. The relationship between the tenant and the landlord is called a tenancy, and the right to possession by the tenant is sometimes called a leasehold interest.
   a. Robinson-Patman Act
   b. Model Code of Professional Responsibility
   c. Lease
   d. Federal Sentencing Guidelines

45. A _____ estate is an ownership interest in land in which a lessee or a tenant holds real property by some form of title from a lessor or landlord.

   _____ is a form of property tenure where one party buys the right to occupy land or a building for a given length of time. As lease is a legal estate, _____ estate can be bought and sold on the open market.

   a. Real Estate Investment Trust
   b. Liquidation value
   c. 3M Company
   d. Leasehold

46. A _____ is a set of exclusive rights granted by a state to an inventor or his assignee for a limited period of time in exchange for a disclosure of an invention.

   The procedure for granting _____s, the requirements placed on the _____ee and the extent of the exclusive rights vary widely between countries according to national laws and international agreements. Typically, however, a _____ application must include one or more claims defining the invention which must be new, inventive, and useful or industrially applicable.

   a. FLSA
   b. Trust indenture
   c. Patent
   d. Negligence

47. An _____ is a term used in behavioral economics to describe those types of behaviors that impose costs on a person in the long-run that are not taken into account when making decisions in the present. Classical Economics discourages government from creating legislation that targets internalities, because it is assumed that the consumer takes these personal costs into account when paying for the good that causes the _____. For example, cigarettes should be taxed because of the negative consumption externalities that they impose, such as second-hand smoke, not because the smoker harms him or herself by smoking.
   a. Operating budget
   b. Authorised capital
   c. Inventory turnover ratio
   d. Internality

48. In accounting and organizational theory, _____ is defined as a process effected by an organization's structure, work and authority flows, people and management information systems, designed to help the organization accomplish specific goals or objectives. It is a means by which an organization's resources are directed, monitored, and measured. It plays an important role in preventing and detecting fraud and protecting the organization's resources, both physical (e.g., machinery and property) and intangible (e.g., reputation or intellectual property such as trademarks.)
   a. Audit risk
   b. Internal control
   c. Audit committee
   d. Auditor independence

Chapter 8. Reporting and Analyzing Long-Term Assets

49. The _____ of 2002 (Pub.L. 107-204, 116 Stat. 745, enacted July 30, 2002), also known as the Public Company Accounting Reform and Investor Protection Act of 2002, is a United States federal law enacted on July 30, 2002 in response to a number of major corporate and accounting scandals including those affecting Enron, Tyco International, Adelphia, Peregrine Systems and WorldCom. The legislation establishes new or enhanced standards for all U.S. public company boards, management, and public accounting firms. It does not apply to privately held companies.

a. FCPA
b. Lease
c. Fair Labor Standards Act
d. Sarbanes-Oxley Act

50. A _____ is the name which a business trades under for commercial purposes, although its registered, legal name, used for contracts and other formal situations, may be another. Pharmaceuticals also have _____s, often dissimilar to their chemical names

Trading names are sometimes registered as trademarks or are regarded as brands.

a. Trade name
b. Consumer-to-business
c. Fund accounting
d. Price variance

51. A _____ or trade mark, identified by the symbols â„¢ (not yet registered) and Â® (registered), is a distinctive sign or indicator used by an individual, business organization or other legal entity to identify that the products and/or services to consumers with which the _____ appears originate from a unique source, and to distinguish its products or services from those of other entities. A _____ is a type of intellectual property, and typically a name, word, phrase, logo, symbol, design, image, or a combination of these elements. There is also a range of non-conventional _____s comprising marks which do not fall into these standard categories.

a. Kanban
b. Trademark
c. FIFO
d. Risk management

52. _____ is a business, economics or investment term that refers to an asset's ability to be easily converted through an act of buying or selling without causing a significant movement in the price and with minimum loss of value. Money, or cash on hand, is the most liquid asset. An act of exchange of a less liquid asset with a more liquid asset is called liquidation.

a. Transfer agent
b. Market liquidity
c. Financial instruments
d. Spot rate

53. _____ is a financial ratio that measures the efficiency of a company's use of its assets in generating sales revenue or sales income to the company.

$$Asset\ Turnover = \frac{Sales}{Average Total Assets}$$

- 'Sales' is the value of 'Net Sales' or 'Sales' from the company's income statement
- 'Average Total Assets' is the value of 'Total assets' from the company's balance sheet in the beginning and the end of the fiscal period divided by 2.

a. Average propensity to consume
b. Asset turnover
c. Information ratio
d. Enterprise Value/Sales

54. The _____, a ratio that is typically applied to banks, in simple terms is defined as expenses as a percentage of revenue (expenses / revenue), with a few variations. A lower percentage is better since that means expenses are low and earnings are high. It is related to operating leverage, which measures the ratio between fixed costs and variable costs.

   a. Operating leverage
   b. Equity ratio
   c. Average rate of return
   d. Efficiency ratio

Chapter 9. Reporting and Analyzing Current Liabilities

1. In accounting, _____ are considered liabilities of the business that are to be settled in cash within the fiscal year or the operating cycle, whichever period is longer.

For example accounts payable for goods, services or supplies that were purchased for use in the operation of the business and payable within a normal period of time would be _____.

Bonds, mortgages and loans that are payable over a term exceeding one year would be fixed liabilities.

   a. Treasury stock   b. Payroll
   c. Closing entries   d. Current liabilities

2. In financial accounting, a _____ is defined as an obligation of an entity arising from past transactions or events, the settlement of which may result in the transfer or use of assets, provision of services or other yielding of economic benefits in the future.
   a. Vested   b. False Claims Act
   c. Corporate governance   d. Liability

3. In economic models, the _____ time frame assumes no fixed factors of production. Firms can enter or leave the marketplace, and the cost (and availability) of land, labor, raw materials, and capital goods can be assumed to vary. In contrast, in the short-run time frame, certain factors are assumed to be fixed, because there is not sufficient time for them to change.
   a. 3M Company   b. BMC Software, Inc.
   c. Short-run   d. Long-run

4. _____ are liabilities with a future benefit over one year, such as notes payable that mature greater than one year.

In accounting, the _____ are shown on the right wing of the balance-sheet representing the sources of funds, which are generally bounded in form of capital assets.

Examples of _____ are debentures, mortgage loans and other bank loans (note: not all bank loans are long term as not all are paid over a period greater than a year, the example is bridging loan.)

   a. Gross sales   b. Book value
   c. Cash basis accounting   d. Long-term liabilities

5. _____ is a term used in subtly different ways in a number of fields, including philosophy, physics, statistics, economics, finance, insurance, psychology, sociology, engineering, and information science. It applies to predictions of future events, to physical measurements already made, or to the unknown.

In his seminal work Risk, _____, and Profit University of Chicago economist Frank Knight (1921) established the important distinction between risk and _____:

> '_____ must be taken in a sense radically distinct from the familiar notion of risk, from which it has never been properly separated....

a. AIG
b. AMEX
c. ABC Television Network
d. Uncertainty

6. _____ is a file or account that contains money that a person or company owes to suppliers, but has not paid yet (a form of debt.) When you receive an invoice you add it to the file, and then you remove it when you pay. Thus, the A/P is a form of credit that suppliers offer to their purchasers by allowing them to pay for a product or service after it has already been received.

a. Accounts receivable
b. Earnings before interest, taxes, depreciation and amortization
c. Accounts payable
d. Accrual

7. A _____ is the pinnacle activity involved in selling products or services in return for money or other compensation. It is an act of completion of a commercial activity.

A _____ is completed by the seller, the owner of the goods.

a. Sale
b. Tertiary sector of economy
c. High yield stock
d. Maturity

8. The _____ is a private, not-for-profit organization whose primary purpose is to develop generally accepted accounting principles (GAAP) within the United States in the public's interest. The Securities and Exchange Commission (SEC) designated the _____ as the organization responsible for setting accounting standards for public companies in the U.S. It was created in 1973, replacing the Accounting Principles Board and the Committee on Accounting Procedure of the American Institute of Certified Public Accountants. The _____'s mission is 'to establish and improve standards of financial accounting and reporting for the guidance and education of the public, including issuers, auditors, and users of financial information.'

The _____ is not a governmental body.

a. Governmental Accounting Standards Board
b. Fannie Mae
c. Public company
d. Financial Accounting Standards Board

9. A _____, also referred to as a note payable in accounting, is a contract where one party (the maker or issuer) makes an unconditional promise in writing to pay a sum of money to the other (the payee), either at a fixed or determinable future time or on demand of the payee, under specific terms. They differ from IOUs in that they contain a specific promise to pay, rather than simply acknowledging that a debt exists.

The terms of a note typically include the principal amount, the interest rate if any, and the maturity date.

a. Promissory note
b. 3M Company
c. BMC Software, Inc.
d. BNSF Railway

10. A _____ is the transfer of wealth from one party (such as a person or company) to another. A _____ is usually made in exchange for the provision of goods, services or both, or to fulfill a legal obligation.

The simplest and oldest form of _____ is barter, the exchange of one good or service for another.

Chapter 9. Reporting and Analyzing Current Liabilities

a. 3M Company
b. BMC Software, Inc.
c. Payee
d. Payment

11. In economics, the concept of the _____ refers to the decision-making time frame of a firm in which at least one factor of production is fixed. Costs which are fixed in the _____ have no impact on a firms decisions. For example a firm can raise output by increasing the amount of labour through overtime.
    a. Long-run
    b. Short-run
    c. BMC Software, Inc.
    d. 3M Company

12. _____, in accrual accounting, (e.g. advance payment received from a client) is, according to revenue recognition, revenue not earned until the delivery of goods or services, which until then, is still owed to the payer, hence remaining a liability.

    _____, sometimes referred to as deferred revenue or unearned revenue, shares characteristics with accrued expense with the difference that a liability to be covered latter is cash received FROM a counterpart, while goods or services are to be delivered in a latter period, when such income item is earned, the related revenue item is recognized, and the same amount is deducted from deferred revenues.
    a. Deferred income
    b. Matching principle
    c. Treasury stock
    d. Gross sales

13. In accounting, _____ or carrying value is the value of an asset according to its balance sheet account balance. For assets, the value is based on the original cost of the asset less any depreciation, amortization or impairment costs made against the asset. Traditionally, a company's _____ is its total assets minus intangible assets and liabilities.
    a. Book value
    b. Depreciation
    c. Generally accepted accounting principles
    d. Matching principle

14. An _____ is a period with reference to which United Kingdom corporation tax is charged. It helps dictate when tax is paid on income and gains. An _____ begins whenever a company comes within the corporation tax charge, and whenever an _____ ends without the company ceasing to be within the charge.
    a. AIG
    b. AMEX
    c. Accounting period
    d. ABC Television Network

15. In accounting/accountancy, _____ are journal entries usually made at the end of an accounting period to allocate income and expenditure to the period in which they actually occurred. The revenue recognition principle is the basis of making _____ that pertain to unearned and accrued revenues under accrual-basis accounting. They are sometimes called Balance Day adjustments because they are made on balance day.
    a. Accrued expense
    b. Earnings before interest, taxes, depreciation and amortization
    c. Accrual
    d. Adjusting entries

16. In accounting, _____ has a very specific meaning. It is an outflow of cash or other valuable assets from a person or company to another person or company. This outflow of cash is generally one side of a trade for products or services that have equal or better current or future value to the buyer than to the seller.

a. ABC Television Network
b. AMEX
c. AIG
d. Expense

17. _____ is the value of a coin, stamp or paper money, as printed on the coin, stamp or bill itself by the minting authority. While the _____ usually refers to the true value of the coin, stamp or bill in question (as with circulation coins) it can sometimes be largely symbolic, as is often the case with bullion coins. For example, a one troy ounce (31 g) American Gold Eagle bullion coin was worth and sold for about $670 USD during 2006 market prices (as of July 17, 2006) and yet has a _____ of only $50 USD.
a. 3M Company
b. BMC Software, Inc.
c. BNSF Railway
d. Face value

18. _____ is a fee paid on borrowed assets. It is the price paid for the use of borrowed money, or, money earned by deposited funds. Assets that are sometimes lent with _____ include money, shares, consumer goods through hire purchase, major assets such as aircraft, and even entire factories in finance lease arrangements. The _____ is calculated upon the value of the assets in the same manner as upon money.
a. Insolvency
b. AIG
c. Interest
d. ABC Television Network

19. _____ relates to the cost of borrowing money. It is the price that a lender charges a borrower for the use of the lender's money. _____ is different from OPEX and CAPEX, for it relates to the capital structure of a company.
a. Interest
b. ABC Television Network
c. AIG
d. Interest expense

20. A _____, in business matters, is an entity that is controlled by a bigger and more powerful entity. The controlled entity is called a company, corporation, or limited liability company, and the controlling entity is called its parent (or the parent company.) The reason for this distinction is that a lone company cannot be a _____ of any organization; only an entity representing a legal fiction as a separate entity can be a _____.
a. BMC Software, Inc.
b. Parent company
c. 3M Company
d. Subsidiary

21. The _____ is a subset of the general ledger used in accounting. The _____ shows detail for part of the accounting records such as property and equipment, prepaid expenses, etc. The detail would include such items as date the item was purchased or expense incurred, a description of the item, the original balance, and the net book value.
a. Credit memo
b. Remittance advice
c. Minority interest
d. Subledger

22. _____ is the process of matching and comparing figures from accounting records against those presented on a bank statement. Less any items which have no relation to the bank statement, the balance of the accounting ledger should reconcile (match) to the balance of the bank statement.

_____ allows companies or individuals to compare their account records to the bank's records of their account balance in order to uncover any possible discrepancies.

a. Bank reconciliation
b. Credit memo
c. Bankruptcy prediction
d. Lower of Cost or Market

Chapter 9. Reporting and Analyzing Current Liabilities

23. A _____ is a type of debt Like all debt instruments, a _____ entails the redistribution of financial assets over time, between the lender and the borrower.
    a. Loan
    b. Lender
    c. Loan to value
    d. Debenture

24. Employment is a contract between two parties, one being the employer and the other being the _____. An _____ may be defined as: 'A person in the service of another under any contract of hire, express or implied, oral or written, where the employer has the power or right to control and direct the _____ in the material details of how the work is to be performed.' Black's Law Dictionary page 471 (5th ed. 1979.)
    a. AIG
    b. Employee
    c. AMEX
    d. ABC Television Network

25. A _____ is a form of periodic payment from an employer to an employee, which may be specified in an employment contract. It is contrasted with piece wages, where each job, hour or other unit is paid separately, rather than on a periodic basis.

    From the point of a view of running a business, _____ can also be viewed as the cost of acquiring human resources for running operations, and is then termed personnel expense or _____ expense.

    a. 3M Company
    b. BMC Software, Inc.
    c. Separation of duties
    d. Salary

26. An _____ is a term used in behavioral economics to describe those types of behaviors that impose costs on a person in the long-run that are not taken into account when making decisions in the present. Classical Economics discourages government from creating legislation that targets internalities, because it is assumed that the consumer takes these personal costs into account when paying for the good that causes the _____. For example, cigarettes should be taxed because of the negative consumption externalities that they impose, such as second-hand smoke, not because the smoker harms him or herself by smoking.
    a. Inventory turnover ratio
    b. Authorised capital
    c. Operating budget
    d. Internality

27. In accounting and organizational theory, _____ is defined as a process effected by an organization's structure, work and authority flows, people and management information systems, designed to help the organization accomplish specific goals or objectives. It is a means by which an organization's resources are directed, monitored, and measured. It plays an important role in preventing and detecting fraud and protecting the organization's resources, both physical (e.g., machinery and property) and intangible (e.g., reputation or intellectual property such as trademarks.)
    a. Audit risk
    b. Auditor independence
    c. Audit committee
    d. Internal control

28. _____ is a cornerstone of accrual accounting together with the revenue recognition principle. They both determine the accounting period, in which revenues and expenses are recognized. According to the principle, expenses are recognized when obligations are (1) incurred (usually when goods are transferred or services rendered, e.g. sold), and (2) offset against recognized revenues, which were generated from those expenses (related on the cause-and-effect basis), no matter when cash is paid out.

Chapter 9. Reporting and Analyzing Current Liabilities

a. Current liabilities
b. Net sales
c. Payroll
d. Matching principle

29. _____ is the remaining amount after deductions from the gross salary, where net means ultimate.

Example deductions: income taxes, trade union dues, authorized deduction for a retirement fund.

_____ is the amount left over after deductions from the gross salary.

a. Round-tripping
b. Net pay
c. 3M Company
d. Residual value

30. In a company, _____ is the sum of all financial records of salaries, wages, bonuses and deductions.

A paycheck, is traditionally a paper document issued by an employer to pay an employee for services rendered. While most commonly used in the United States, recently the physical paycheck has been increasingly replaced by electronic direct deposit to bank accounts.

a. 3M Company
b. Total Expense Ratio
c. Tax expense
d. Payroll

31. _____ generally refers to two kinds of taxes: Taxes which employers are required to withhold from employees' pay Pay-As-You-Earn or Pay-As-You-Go tax; and taxes which are paid from the employer's own funds and which are directly related to employing a worker, which may be either fixed charges or proportionally linked to an employee's pay.

In Australia, the _____ is a specific tax which is paid to states and territories by employers, not by employees. The tax is not deducted from the worker's pay.

a. Federal Unemployment Tax Act
b. Passive foreign investment company
c. Nonbusiness Energy Property Tax Credit
d. Payroll tax

32. The _____ tax is a United States payroll tax imposed by the federal government on both employees and employers to fund Social Security and Medicare --federal programs that provide benefits for retirees, the disabled, and children of deceased workers. Social Security benefits include old-age, survivors, and disability insurance (OASDI); Medicare provides hospital insurance benefits. The amount that one pays in payroll taxes throughout one's working career is indirectly tied to the social security benefits annuity that one receives as a retiree.

a. Deficit
b. Federal Insurance Contributions Act
c. Tax protester Sixteenth Amendment arguments
d. Windfall profits tax

33. _____, in law and economics, is a form of risk management primarily used to hedge against the risk of a contingent loss. _____ is defined as the equitable transfer of the risk of a loss, from one entity to another, in exchange for a premium, and can be thought of as a guaranteed small loss to prevent a large, possibly devastating loss. An insurer is a company selling the _____; an insured is the person or entity buying the _____.

a. AIG
b. AMEX
c. ABC Television Network
d. Insurance

Chapter 9. Reporting and Analyzing Current Liabilities

34. The _____ is the United States federal government agency that collects taxes and enforces the internal revenue laws. It is an agency within the U.S. Dept of the treasury responsible for interpretation and application of Federal tax law. The official U.S. Treasury regulations provide (in part):

The _____ is a bureau of the Department of the Treasury under the immediate direction of the Commissioner of Internal Revenue.

a. Use tax
c. Income tax
b. Indirect tax
d. Internal Revenue Service

35. A _____ is a fungible, negotiable instrument representing financial value. they are broadly categorized into debt securities (such as banknotes, bonds and debentures), and equity securities; e.g., common stocks. The company or other entity issuing the _____ is called the issuer.

a. 3M Company
c. BMC Software, Inc.
b. Tracking stock
d. Security

36. _____ in the United States currently refers to the federal Old-Age, Survivors, and Disability Insurance (OASDI) program.

The original _____ Act and the current version of the Act, as amended encompass several social welfare and social insurance programs. The larger and better known programs are:

- Federal Old-Age, Survivors, and Disability Insurance
- Unemployment benefits
- Temporary Assistance for Needy Families
- Health Insurance for Aged and Disabled (Medicare)
- Grants to States for Medical Assistance Programs (Medicaid)
- State Children's Health Insurance Program (SCHIP)
- Supplemental Security Income (Social SecurityI)

U.S. _____ is a social insurance program funded through dedicated payroll taxes called Federal Insurance Contributions Act (FICA.) Tax deposits are formally entrusted to Federal Old-Age and Survivors Insurance Trust Fund, or Federal Disability Insurance Trust Fund, Federal Hospital Insurance Trust Fund or the Federal Supplementary Medical Insurance Trust Fund.

a. Comparable
c. Social Security
b. Sale
d. Price-to-sales ratio

37. The United States _____ is an independent agency of the United States federal government that administers Social Security, a social insurance program consisting of retirement, disability, and survivors' benefits. To qualify for these benefits, most American workers pay Social Security taxes on their earnings; future benefits are based on the employees' contributions.

The _____ was established by a law currently codified at 42 U.S.C.

a. Time value of money
b. Minority interest
c. Return on assets
d. Social Security Administration

38. The _____ is a United States federal law that imposes a federal employer tax used to fund state workforce agencies. Employers report this tax by filing an annual Form 940 with the Internal Revenue Service.

a. Federal Unemployment Tax Act
b. Council Tax
c. Transfer tax
d. Tax evasion

39. _____ is an amount withheld by the party making a payment to another (payee) and paid to the taxation authorities. The amount the payer deducts may vary, depending on the nature of the product or service being paid for. The payee is assessed on the gross amount, and the tax to be withheld (the _____) is computed in that assessment.

a. Salaries tax
b. Tax advantage
c. Tax wedge
d. Withholding tax

40. An _____ is a tax levied on the financial income of people, corporations, or other legal entities. Various _____ systems exist, with varying degrees of tax incidence. Income taxation can be progressive, proportional, or regressive.

a. Ordinary income
b. Implied level of government service
c. Income tax
d. Individual Retirement Arrangement

41. _____, is a liability with an uncertain timing or amount, but where the uncertainty is not significant enough to qualify it as a provision. An example is an unpaid obligation to pay for goods or services received FROM a counterpart, while cash for them is to be paid out in a latter accounting period when its amount is deducted from _____s.

a. Assets
b. Accrual basis accounting
c. Accrued expense
d. Accounts receivable

42. The _____ (or _____, 26 U.S.C. ch.23) is a United States federal law that imposes a federal employer tax used to fund state workforce agencies. Employers report this tax by filing an annual Form 940 with the Internal Revenue Service.

a. Fuel tax
b. Carbon tax
c. FUTA
d. Form 1099

43. _____ refers to the methods, practices and operations conducted to promote and sustain certain categories of commercial activity. The term is understood to have different specific meanings depending on the context. Merchandise is a sale goods at a store

In marketing, one of the definitions of _____ is the practice in which the brand or image from one product or service is used to sell another.

a. Merchandise
b. 3M Company
c. BMC Software, Inc.
d. Merchandising

Chapter 9. Reporting and Analyzing Current Liabilities

44. The _____ of 2002 (Pub.L. 107-204, 116 Stat. 745, enacted July 30, 2002), also known as the Public Company Accounting Reform and Investor Protection Act of 2002, is a United States federal law enacted on July 30, 2002 in response to a number of major corporate and accounting scandals including those affecting Enron, Tyco International, Adelphia, Peregrine Systems and WorldCom. The legislation establishes new or enhanced standards for all U.S. public company boards, management, and public accounting firms. It does not apply to privately held companies.
   a. FCPA
   b. Fair Labor Standards Act
   c. Lease
   d. Sarbanes-Oxley Act

45. A _____ is a compensation, usually financial, received by a worker in exchange for their labor.

Compensation in terms of _____s is given to worker and compensation in terms of salary is given to employees. Compensation is a monetary benefits given to employees in returns of the services provided by them.

   a. Wage
   b. Retirement plan
   c. BMC Software, Inc.
   d. 3M Company

46. In business and accounting, _____ are everything of value that is owned by a person or company. It is a claim on the property your income of a borrower. The balance sheet of a firm records the monetary value of the _____ owned by the firm.
   a. Accounts receivable
   b. Assets
   c. Accrual basis accounting
   d. Earnings before interest, taxes, depreciation and amortization

47. _____ and benefits in kind are various non-wage compensations provided to employees in addition to their normal wages or salaries. Where an employee exchanges (cash) wages for some other form of benefit, this is generally referred to as a 'salary sacrifice' arrangement. In most countries, most kinds of _____ are taxable to at least some degree.
   a. Employee benefits
   b. AMEX
   c. AIG
   d. ABC Television Network

48. _____ is that which is owed; usually referencing assets owed, but the term can also cover moral obligations and other interactions not requiring money. In the case of assets, _____ is a means of using future purchasing power in the present before a summation has been earned. Some companies and corporations use _____ as a part of their overall corporate finance strategy.
   a. Debenture
   b. Loan
   c. Lender
   d. Debt

49. An _____ is quite usually a standard guarantee from the seller of a product that specifies the extent to which the quality or performance of the product is assured and states the conditions under which the product can be returned, replaced, or repaired. It is often given in the form of a specific, written 'Warranty' document. However, a warranty may also arise by operation of law based upon the seller's description of the goods, and perhaps their source and quality, and any material deviation from that specification would violate the guarantee.
   a. Exclusive right
   b. Operating Lease
   c. Escheat
   d. Express warranty

Chapter 9. Reporting and Analyzing Current Liabilities

50. _____ that may or may not be incurred by an entity depending on the outcome of a future event such as a court case. These liabilities are recorded in a company's accounts and shown in the balance sheet when both probable and reasonably estimable. A footnote to the balance sheet describes the nature and extent of the _____.
- a. Headnote
- b. Tangible
- c. Contingent liabilities
- d. Nonacquiescence

51. _____ is a survey-based economic technique for the valuation of non-market resources, such as environmental preservation or the impact of contamination. While these resources do give people utility, certain aspects of them do not have a market price as they are not directly sold--for example, people receive benefit from a beautiful view of a mountain, but it would be tough to value using price-based models. _____ surveys are one technique which is used to measure these aspects.
- a. 3M Company
- b. BMC Software, Inc.
- c. Contingent valuation
- d. BNSF Railway

52. In finance, _____ is the process of estimating the potential market value of a financial asset or liability. They can be done on assets (for example, investments in marketable securities such as stocks, options, business enterprises, or intangible assets such as patents and trademarks) or on liabilities (e.g., Bonds issued by a company.) A _____ is required in many contexts including investment analysis, capital budgeting, merger and acquisition transactions, financial reporting, taxable events to determine the proper tax liability, and in litigation.
- a. Vyborg Appeal
- b. Daybook
- c. Valuation
- d. Disclosure

53. _____, also known as property, plant, and equipment (PP&E), is a term used in accountancy for assets and property which cannot easily be converted into cash. This can be compared with current assets such as cash or bank accounts, which are described as liquid assets. In most cases, only tangible assets are referred to as fixed.
- a. Minority interest
- b. Subledger
- c. Fixed asset
- d. Bankruptcy prediction

54. In finance, or business _____ is the ability of an entity to pay its debts with available cash. _____ can also be described as the ability of a corporation to meet its long-term fixed expenses and to accomplish long-term expansion and growth. The better a company's _____, the better it is financially.
- a. 3M Company
- b. BMC Software, Inc.
- c. Capital asset
- d. Solvency

55. _____ or interest coverage ratio is a measure of a company's ability to honor its debt payments. It may be calculated as either EBIT or EBITDA divided by the total interest payable.

- a. Capital recovery factor
- b. Yield Gap
- c. Times interest earned
- d. Return of capital

Chapter 9. Reporting and Analyzing Current Liabilities 99

56. A _____ has several related meanings:

- a daily record of events or business; a private _____ is usually referred to as a diary.
- a newspaper or other periodical, in the literal sense of one published each day;
- many publications issued at stated intervals, such as magazines, or scholarly academic _____s, or the record of the transactions of a society, are often called _____s. Although _____ is sometimes used, erroneously, as a synonym for 'magazine,' in academic use, a _____ refers to a serious, scholarly publication, most often peer-reviewed. A non-scholarly magazine written for an educated audience about an industry or an area of professional activity is usually called a professional magazine.

The word 'journalist' for one whose business is writing for the public press has been in use since the end of the 17th century.

Open access _____s are scholarly _____s that are available to the reader without financial or other barrier other than access to the internet itself. Some are subsidized, and some require payment on behalf of the author. Subsidized _____s are financed by an academic institution or a government information center.

a. BMC Software, Inc.
c. Journal
b. BNSF Railway
d. 3M Company

57. _____ refers to the computer-based systems used to perform financial transactions electronically.

The term is used for a number of different concepts:

- Cardholder-initiated transactions, where a cardholder makes use of a payment card
- Direct deposit payroll payments for a business to its employees, possibly via a payroll services company
- Direct debit payments from customer to business, where the transaction is initiated by the business with customer permission
- Electronic bill payment in online banking, which may be delivered by _____ or paper check
- Transactions involving stored value of electronic money, possibly in a private currency
- Wire transfer via an international banking network (generally carries a higher fee)
- Electronic Benefit Transfer

electronic funds transferPOS (short for _____ at Point of Sale) is an Australian and New Zealand electronic processing system for credit cards, debit cards and charge cards.

European banks and card companies also sometimes reference 'electronic funds transferPOS' as the system used for processing card transactions through terminals on points of sale, though the system is not the trademarked Australian/New Zealand variant.

Credit cards

_____ may be initiated by a cardholder when a payment card such as a credit card or debit card is used.

a. ABC Television Network
b. AMEX
c. AIG
d. Electronic funds transfer

58. _____ is a specific term used in companies' financial reporting from the company-whole point of view. Because that use excludes the effects of changing ownership interest, an economic measure of _____ is necessary for financial analysis from the shareholders' point of view

_____ is defined by the Financial Accounting Standards Board, or FASB, as 'the change in equity [net assets] of a business enterprise during a period from transactions and other events and circumstances from nonowner sources. It includes all changes in equity during a period except those resulting from investments by owners and distributions to owners.'

_____ is the sum of net income and other items that must bypass the income statement because they have not been realized, including items like an unrealized holding gain or loss from available for sale securities and foreign currency translation gains or losses.

a. BMC Software, Inc.
b. BNSF Railway
c. 3M Company
d. Comprehensive income

59. _____, in accrual accounting, is any account where the asset or liability is not realized until a future date (accounting period), e.g. annuities, charges, taxes, income, etc. The _____ item may be carried, dependent on type of deferral, as either an asset or liability.
a. Deferred
b. Cash basis accounting
c. Pro forma
d. Payroll

60. _____ is the term used to refer to the standard framework of guidelines for financial accounting used in any given jurisdiction. _____ includes the standards, conventions, and rules accountants follow in recording and summarizing transactions, and in the preparation of financial statements.

Financial accounting information must be assembled and reported objectively.

a. Current asset
b. Long-term liabilities
c. General ledger
d. Generally accepted accounting principles

Chapter 10. Reporting and Analyzing Long-Term Liabilities

1. In economic models, the _____ time frame assumes no fixed factors of production. Firms can enter or leave the marketplace, and the cost (and availability) of land, labor, raw materials, and capital goods can be assumed to vary. In contrast, in the short-run time frame, certain factors are assumed to be fixed, because there is not sufficient time for them to change.
   a. 3M Company
   b. BMC Software, Inc.
   c. Long-run
   d. Short-run

2. _____ are liabilities with a future benefit over one year, such as notes payable that mature greater than one year.

In accounting, the _____ are shown on the right wing of the balance-sheet representing the sources of funds, which are generally bounded in form of capital assets.

Examples of _____ are debentures, mortgage loans and other bank loans (note: not all bank loans are long term as not all are paid over a period greater than a year, the example is bridging loan.)

   a. Gross sales
   b. Book value
   c. Cash basis accounting
   d. Long-term liabilities

3. In financial accounting, a _____ is defined as an obligation of an entity arising from past transactions or events, the settlement of which may result in the transfer or use of assets, provision of services or other yielding of economic benefits in the future.
   a. Vested
   b. Corporate governance
   c. False Claims Act
   d. Liability

4. In finance, a _____ is a debt security, in which the authorized issuer owes the holders a debt and, depending on the terms of the _____, is obliged to pay interest (the coupon) and/or to repay the principal at a later date, termed maturity. It is a formal contract to repay borrowed money with interest at fixed intervals.

Thus a _____ is like a loan: the issuer is the borrower, the _____ holder is the lender, and the coupon is the interest.

   a. Revenue bonds
   b. Zero-coupon bond
   c. Bond
   d. Coupon rate

5. _____ is a fee paid on borrowed assets. It is the price paid for the use of borrowed money , or, money earned by deposited funds .Assets that are sometimes lent with _____ include money, shares, consumer goods through hire purchase, major assets such as aircraft, and even entire factories in finance lease arrangements. The _____ is calculated upon the value of the assets in the same manner as upon money.
   a. ABC Television Network
   b. AIG
   c. Insolvency
   d. Interest

6. _____ is a life of security. It may also refer to the final payment date of a loan or other financial instrument, at which point all remaining interest and principal is due to be paid.

1, 3, 6 months _____ band can be calculated by using 30-day per month periods. For _____ bands over a year it is acceptable to use 365 day per year. For example with a Treasury Bond, its _____ is the date on which the principal is paid.

a. Factor

b. Statements of Financial Accounting Standards No. 133, Accounting for Derivative Instruments and Hedging Activities

c. The Goodyear Tire ' Rubber Company

d. Maturity

7. _____ measures the rate of return on the ownership interest (shareholders' equity) of the common stock owners. It measures a firm's efficiency at generating profits from every dollar of shareholders' equity (also known as net assets or assets minus liabilities.) It shows how well a company uses investment dollars to generate earnings growth.

a. Sortino ratio
b. Like for like
c. Return on capital employed
d. Return on equity

8. NYSE Amex Equities, formerly known as the _____ is an _____ situated in New York. AMEX was a mutual organization, owned by its members. Until 1953 it was known as the New York Curb Exchange.

a. AIG
b. American Stock Exchange
c. ABC Television Network
d. AMEX

9. _____ is that which is owed; usually referencing assets owed, but the term can also cover moral obligations and other interactions not requiring money. In the case of assets, _____ is a means of using future purchasing power in the present before a summation has been earned. Some companies and corporations use _____ as a part of their overall corporate finance strategy.

a. Lender
b. Loan
c. Debenture
d. Debt

10. _____ is an equity (stock) exchange located at 11 Wall Street in lower Manhattan, New York, USA.) It is the largest stock exchange in the world by dollar value of its listed companies' securities. As of October 2008, the combined capitalization of all domestic _____ listed companies was US$10.1 trillion.

a. New York Stock Exchange
b. 3M Company
c. BNSF Railway
d. BMC Software, Inc.

11. _____, in finance and accounting, means stated value or face value. From this comes the expressions at par (at the _____), over par (over _____) and under par (under _____).

_____ is a nominal value of a security which is determined by an issuer company at a minimum price. _____ of an equity (a stock) is a somewhat archaic concept. The _____ of a stock was the share price upon initial offering; the issuing company promised not to issue further shares below _____, so investors could be confident that no one else was receiving a more favorable issue price. This was far more important in unregulated equity markets than in the regulated markets that exist today.

a. Par value
b. Net worth
c. Creditor
d. Restructuring

12. A _____, (formerly a securities exchange) is a corporation or mutual organization which provides 'trading' facilities for stock brokers and traders, to trade stocks and other securities. _____s also provide facilities for the issue and redemption of securities as well as other financial instruments and capital events including the payment of income and dividends. The securities traded on a _____ include: shares issued by companies, unit trusts, derivatives, pooled investment products and bonds.

Chapter 10. Reporting and Analyzing Long-Term Liabilities

a. 3M Company
c. BNSF Railway
b. BMC Software, Inc.
d. Stock Exchange

13. _____ is a legal document issued to lenders and describes key terms such as the interest rate, maturity date, convertibility, pledge, promises, representations, covenants, and other terms of the bond offering. When the Offering Memorandum is prepared in advance of marketing a Bond, the indenture will typically be summarised in the 'Description of Notes' section.

a. Leasing
c. Bond indenture
b. Malpractice
d. Consumer protection laws

14. Discounting is a financial mechanism in which a debtor obtains the right to delay payments to a creditor, for a defined period of time, in exchange for a charge or fee. Essentially, the party that owes money in the present purchases the right to delay the payment until some future date. The _____, or charge, is simply the difference between the original amount owed in the present and the amount that has to be paid in the future to settle the debt.

a. Risk aversion
c. Discounting
b. Discount factor
d. Discount

15. A _____ is a bond bought at a price lower than its face value, with the face value repaid at the time of maturity. It does not make periodic interest payments, or so-called 'coupons,' hence the term _____. Investors earn return from the compounded interest all paid at maturity plus the difference between the discounted price of the bond and its par value.

a. Callable bond
c. Municipal bond
b. Premium bond
d. Zero-coupon bond

16. A _____ is like a lottery bond issued by the United Kingdom government's National Savings and Investments scheme. The government promises to buy back the bond, on request, for its original price.

_____s were introduced by the government in 1956, with the aim of encouraging saving and controlling inflation, with the first bonds going on sale on 1 November of that year.

a. Callable bond
c. Revenue bonds
b. Zero-coupon bond
d. Premium bond

17. An _____ is a legal contract between two parties, particularly for indentured labour or a term of apprenticeship but also for certain land transactions. The term comes from the medieval English '_____ of retainer' -- a legal contract written in duplicate on the same sheet, with the copies separated by cutting along a jagged line so that the teeth of the two parts could later be refitted to confirm authenticity. Each party to the deed would then retain a part.

a. Impracticability
c. Employee Retirement Income Security Act
b. Operating Lease
d. Indenture

18. In marketing a _____ is a ticket or document that can be exchanged for a financial discount or rebate when purchasing a product. Customarily, _____s are issued by manufacturers of consumer packaged goods or by retailers, to be used in retail stores as a part of sales promotions. They are often widely distributed through mail, magazines, newspapers, the Internet, and mobile devices such as cell phones.

a. 3M Company
c. Merchandising
b. BMC Software, Inc.
d. Coupon

Chapter 10. Reporting and Analyzing Long-Term Liabilities

19. The _____ of a bond is the amount of interest paid per year expressed as a percentage of the face value of the bond. It is the interest rate that a bond issuer will pay to a bondholder.

For example if you hold $10,000 nominal of a bond described as a 4.5% loan stock, you will receive $450 in interest each year (probably in two installments of $225 each.)

a. Revenue bonds
b. Callable bond
c. Convertible bond
d. Coupon rate

20. In accounting, _____ has a very specific meaning. It is an outflow of cash or other valuable assets from a person or company to another person or company. This outflow of cash is generally one side of a trade for products or services that have equal or better current or future value to the buyer than to the seller.

a. ABC Television Network
b. AIG
c. AMEX
d. Expense

21. _____ is an acronym for First In, First Out, an abstraction in ways of organizing and manipulation of data relative to time and prioritization. This expression describes the principle of a queue processing technique or servicing conflicting demands by ordering process by first-come, first-served (FCFS) behaviour: what comes in first is handled first, what comes in next waits until the first is finished, etc.

Thus it is analogous to the behaviour of persons queueing (or 'standing in line', in common American parlance), where the persons leave the queue in the order they arrive, or waiting one's turn at a traffic control signal.

a. Trademark
b. FIFO
c. Kanban
d. Risk management

22. _____ relates to the cost of borrowing money. It is the price that a lender charges a borrower for the use of the lender's money. _____ is different from OPEX and CAPEX, for it relates to the capital structure of a company.

a. Interest
b. AIG
c. Interest expense
d. ABC Television Network

23. In economics, a _____ is a lower rated, potentially higher paying bond.

- High-yield debt

A high-risk, non-investment-grade bond with a low credit rating, usually BB or lower; as a consequence, it usually has a high yield. opposite of investment-grade bond. This content can be found on the following page:

a. BMC Software, Inc.
b. 3M Company
c. BNSF Railway
d. Junk bond

24. A _____ is any one of a variety of different systems, institutions, procedures, social relations and infrastructures whereby persons trade, and goods and services are exchanged, forming part of the economy. It is an arrangement that allows buyers and sellers to exchange things. _____s vary in size, range, geographic scale, location, types and variety of human communities, as well as the types of goods and services traded.

Chapter 10. Reporting and Analyzing Long-Term Liabilities

a. Recession
b. Perfect competition
c. Market
d. Market Failure

25. _____ is the process of increasing, or accounting for, an amount over a period of time. Particular instances of the term include:

- _____, the allocation of a lump sum amount to different time periods, particularly for loans and other forms of finance, including related interest or other finance charges.
  - _____ schedule, a table detailing each periodic payment on a loan (typically a mortgage), as generated by an _____ calculator.
  - Negative _____, an _____ schedule where the loan amount actually increases through not paying the full interest
- Amortized analysis, analyzing the execution cost of algorithms over a sequence of operations.
- _____ of capital expenditures of certain assets under accounting rules, particularly intangible assets, in a manner analogous to depreciation.
- _____

a. Intangible
b. Annuity
c. EBIT
d. Amortization

26. In accounting, _____ or carrying value is the value of an asset according to its balance sheet account balance. For assets, the value is based on the original cost of the asset less any depreciation, amortization or impairment costs made against the asset. Traditionally, a company's _____ is its total assets minus intangible assets and liabilities.

a. Matching principle
b. Book value
c. Generally accepted accounting principles
d. Depreciation

27. There are several methods for calculating depreciation, generally based on either the passage of time or the level of activity (or use) of the asset.

_____ is the simplest and most often used technique, in which the company estimates the salvage value of the asset at the end of the period during which it will be used to generate revenues (useful life), and will expense a portion of original cost in equal increments over that period.

a. Closing entries
b. Pro forma
c. Current asset
d. Straight-line depreciation

28. _____ measures the nominal future sum of money that a given sum of money is 'worth' at a specified time in the future assuming a certain interest rate rate of return; it is the present value multiplied by the accumulation function.

The value does not include corrections for inflation or other factors that affect the true value of money in the future. This is used in time value of money calculations.

a. 3M Company
b. Net present value
c. Present value
d. Future value

Chapter 10. Reporting and Analyzing Long-Term Liabilities

29. _____ is the price at which an asset would trade in a competitive Walrasian auction setting. _____ is often used interchangeably with open _____, fair value or fair _____, although these terms have distinct definitions in different standards, and may differ in some circumstances.

International Valuation Standards defines _____ as 'the estimated amount for which a property should exchange on the date of valuation between a willing buyer and a willing seller in an arme;s-length transaction after proper marketing wherein the parties had each acted knowledgeably, prudently, and without compulsion.'

_____ is a concept distinct from market price, which is e;the price at which one can transacte;, while _____ is e;the true underlying valuee; according to theoretical standards.

 a. Debtor
 b. Segregated portfolio company
 c. Sinking fund
 d. Market value

30. _____ is the value on a given date of a future payment or series of future payments, discounted to reflect the time value of money and other factors such as investment risk. _____ calculations are widely used in business and economics to provide a means to compare cash flows at different times on a meaningful 'like to like' basis.

The most commonly applied model of the time value of money is compound interest.

 a. 3M Company
 b. Net present value
 c. Future value
 d. Present value

31. The _____ of 2002 (Pub.L. 107-204, 116 Stat. 745, enacted July 30, 2002), also known as the Public Company Accounting Reform and Investor Protection Act of 2002, is a United States federal law enacted on July 30, 2002 in response to a number of major corporate and accounting scandals including those affecting Enron, Tyco International, Adelphia, Peregrine Systems and WorldCom. The legislation establishes new or enhanced standards for all U.S. public company boards, management, and public accounting firms. It does not apply to privately held companies.
 a. Sarbanes-Oxley Act
 b. Fair Labor Standards Act
 c. FCPA
 d. Lease

32. In finance, the term _____ describes the amount in cash that returns to the owners of a security. Normally it does not include the price variations, at the difference of the total return. _____ applies to various stated rates of return on stocks (common and preferred, and convertible), fixed income instruments (bonds, notes, bills, strips, zero coupon), and some other investment type insurance products (e.g. annuities.)
 a. Pension System
 b. Disclosure
 c. Residence trusts
 d. Yield

33. _____ is one of the four Ps of the marketing mix. The other three aspects are product, promotion, and place. It is also a key variable in microeconomic price allocation theory.
 a. Price
 b. Cost-plus pricing
 c. Target costing
 d. Pricing

Chapter 10. Reporting and Analyzing Long-Term Liabilities

34. A _____ is a financial contract between two parties, the buyer and the seller of this type of option. It is the option to buy shares of stock at a specified time in the future. Often it is simply labeled a 'call'. The buyer of the option has the right, but not the obligation to buy an agreed quantity of a particular commodity or financial instrument (the underlying instrument) from the seller of the option at a certain time (the expiration date) for a certain price (the strike price.)
   a. BMC Software, Inc.
   b. 3M Company
   c. Strike price
   d. Call option

35. A _____ is a type of bond that allows the issuer of the bond to retain the privilege of redeeming the bond at some point before the bond reaches the date of maturity. In other words, on the call dates, the issuer has the right, but not the obligation, to buy back the bonds from the bond holders at the call price. Technically speaking, the bonds are not really bought and held by the issuer but cancelled immediately.
   a. Coupon rate
   b. Callable bond
   c. Catastrophe bonds
   d. Zero-coupon

36. In finance, an _____ is a contract between a buyer and a seller that gives the buyer the right--but not the obligation--to buy or to sell a particular asset (the underlying asset) at a later time at an agreed price. In return for granting the _____, the seller collects a payment (the premium) from the buyer. A call _____ gives the buyer the right to buy the underlying asset; a put _____ gives the buyer of the _____ the right to sell the underlying asset.
   a. ABC Television Network
   b. AIG
   c. Option
   d. AMEX

37. A _____, also referred to as a note payable in accounting, is a contract where one party (the maker or issuer) makes an unconditional promise in writing to pay a sum of money to the other (the payee), either at a fixed or determinable future time or on demand of the payee, under specific terms. They differ from IOUs in that they contain a specific promise to pay, rather than simply acknowledging that a debt exists.

The terms of a note typically include the principal amount, the interest rate if any, and the maturity date.

   a. 3M Company
   b. BMC Software, Inc.
   c. BNSF Railway
   d. Promissory note

38. A _____ is the transfer of an interest in property (or the equivalent in law - a charge) to a lender as a security for a debt - usually a loan of money. While a _____ in itself is not a debt, it is the lender's security for a debt. It is a transfer of an interest in land (or the equivalent) from the owner to the _____ lender, on the condition that this interest will be returned to the owner when the terms of the _____ have been satisfied or performed.
   a. Mortgage
   b. BNSF Railway
   c. 3M Company
   d. BMC Software, Inc.

39. A _____ is the pinnacle activity involved in selling products or services in return for money or other compensation. It is an act of completion of a commercial activity.

A _____ is completed by the seller, the owner of the goods.

   a. Tertiary sector of economy
   b. Sale
   c. High yield stock
   d. Maturity

Chapter 10. Reporting and Analyzing Long-Term Liabilities

40. A _____ is a debt security issued by a business entity, such as a corporation, or by a government. It differs from the more common types of investment securities in that it is unregistered - no records are kept of the owner, or the transactions involving ownership. Whoever physically holds the paper on which the bond is issued owns the instrument.
   a. Bearer bond
   b. Revenue bonds
   c. Coupon rate
   d. Convertible bond

41. In finance, a _____ is a type of bond that can be converted into shares of stock in the issuing company, usually at some pre-announced ratio. It is a hybrid security with debt- and equity-like features. Although it typically has a low coupon rate, the holder is compensated with the ability to convert the bond to common stock, usually at a substantial discount to the stock's market value.
   a. Convertible bond
   b. Coupon rate
   c. Zero-coupon
   d. Zero-coupon bond

42. A _____ is defined as a certificate of agreement of loans which is given under the company's stamp and carries an undertaking that the _____ holder will get a fixed return (fixed on the basis of interest rates) and the principal amount whenever the _____ matures.

In finance, a _____ is a long-term debt instrument used by governments and large companies to obtain funds. It is defined as 'any form of borrowing that commits a firm to pay interest and repay capital.

   a. Loan to value
   b. Credit rating
   c. Loan
   d. Debenture

43. A municipality is an administrative entity composed of a clearly defined territory and its population and commonly denotes a city, town or a small grouping of them. A municipality is typically governed by a mayor and a city council or _____ council.

The notion of municipality includes townships but is not restricted to them.

   a. BNSF Railway
   b. 3M Company
   c. Municipal
   d. BMC Software, Inc.

44. A _____ is a bond issued by a city or other local government, or their agencies. Potential issuers of these include cities, counties, redevelopment agencies, school districts, publicly owned airports and seaports, and any other governmental entity (or group of governments) below the state level. A _____ may be a general obligation of the issuer or secured by specified revenues.
   a. Convertible bond
   b. Zero-coupon
   c. Callable bond
   d. Municipal bond

45. _____ are financial bonds that mature in installments over a period of time. In effect, a $100,000, 5-year serial bond would mature in a $20,000 annuity over a 5-year interval. Bond issues consisting of a series of blocks of securities maturing in sequence, the coupon rate can be different.
   a. Low Income Housing Tax Credit
   b. Just-in-time
   c. Household and Dependent Care Credit
   d. Serial bonds

46. A _____ is a fund established by a government agency or business for the purpose of reducing debt.

The _____ was first used in Great Britain in the 18th century to reduce national debt. While used by Robert Walpole in 1716 and effectively in the 1720s and early 1730s, it originated in the commercial tax syndicates of the Italian peninsula of the 14th century to retire redeemable public debt of those cities.

   a. Treasury company
   c. Sinking fund
   b. Payback period
   d. Segregated portfolio company

47. In finance, or business _____ is the ability of an entity to pay its debts with available cash. _____ can also be described as the ability of a corporation to meet its long-term fixed expenses and to accomplish long-term expansion and growth. The better a company's _____, the better it is financially.
   a. BMC Software, Inc.
   c. Capital asset
   b. 3M Company
   d. Solvency

48. The term _____ is used in finance theory to refer to any terminating stream of fixed payments over a specified period of time. This usage is most commonly seen in academic discussions of finance, usually in connection with the valuation of the stream of payments, taking into account time value of money concepts such as interest rate and future value.

Examples of these are regular deposits to a savings account, monthly home mortgage payments and monthly insurance payments.

   a. Appropriation
   c. Intangible
   b. Improvement
   d. Annuity

49. _____, is a liability with an uncertain timing or amount, but where the uncertainty is not significant enough to qualify it as a provision. An example is an unpaid obligation to pay for goods or services received FROM a counterpart, while cash for them is to be paid out in a latter accounting period when its amount is deducted from _____s.
   a. Accrual basis accounting
   c. Accrued expense
   b. Assets
   d. Accounts receivable

50. In accounting/accountancy, _____ are journal entries usually made at the end of an accounting period to allocate income and expenditure to the period in which they actually occurred. The revenue recognition principle is the basis of making _____ that pertain to unearned and accrued revenues under accrual-basis accounting. They are sometimes called Balance Day adjustments because they are made on balance day.
   a. Accrued expense
   c. Earnings before interest, taxes, depreciation and amortization
   b. Accrual
   d. Adjusting entries

51. In investment, the _____ assesses the credit worthiness of a corporation's debt issues. It is analogous to credit ratings for individuals and countries. The credit rating is a financial indicator to potential investors of debt securities such as bonds.
   a. Market value
   c. Treasury company
   b. Holding gains
   d. Bond credit rating

Chapter 10. Reporting and Analyzing Long-Term Liabilities

52. A _____ is a contract conferring a right on one person to possess property belonging to another person (called a landlord or lessor) to the exclusion of the owner landlord. It is a rental agreement between landlord and tenant. The relationship between the tenant and the landlord is called a tenancy, and the right to possession by the tenant is sometimes called a leasehold interest.
    a. Lease
    b. Federal Sentencing Guidelines
    c. Model Code of Professional Responsibility
    d. Robinson-Patman Act

53. An _____ is a lease whose term is short compared to the useful life of the asset or piece of equipment (an airliner, a ship etc.) being leased. An _____ is commonly used to acquire equipment on a relatively short-term basis.
    a. Express warranty
    b. Operating lease
    c. Issued shares
    d. Employee Retirement Income Security Act

54. In economics, the concept of the _____ refers to the decision-making time frame of a firm in which at least one factor of production is fixed. Costs which are fixed in the _____ have no impact on a firms decisions. For example a firm can raise output by increasing the amount of labour through overtime.
    a. Short-run
    b. Long-run
    c. BMC Software, Inc.
    d. 3M Company

55. The term _____ or superannuation refers to a pension granted upon retirement. They may be set up by employers, insurance companies, the government or other institutions such as employer associations or trade unions.
    a. Wage
    b. Retirement plan
    c. BMC Software, Inc.
    d. 3M Company

56. In economics, _____ or _____ goods or real _____ refers to factors of production used to create goods or services that are not themselves significantly consumed (though they may depreciate) in the production process. _____ goods may be acquired with money or financial _____. In finance and accounting, _____ generally refers to financial wealth, especially that used to start or maintain a business.
    a. Vyborg Appeal
    b. Disclosure
    c. Screening
    d. Capital

57. _____ is a type of lease - the other being an operating lease. A _____ effectively allows a firm to finance the purchase of an asset, even if, strictly speaking, the firm never acquires the asset. Typically, a _____ will give the lessee control over an asset for a large proportion of the asset's useful life, providing them the benefits and risks of ownership.
    a. Debt ratio
    b. 3M Company
    c. Profitability index
    d. Finance lease

58. A _____ is the transfer of wealth from one party (such as a person or company) to another. A _____ is usually made in exchange for the provision of goods, services or both, or to fulfill a legal obligation.

The simplest and oldest form of _____ is barter, the exchange of one good or service for another.

    a. 3M Company
    b. Payment
    c. BMC Software, Inc.
    d. Payee

Chapter 10. Reporting and Analyzing Long-Term Liabilities

59. _____ is a file or account that contains money that a person or company owes to suppliers, but has not paid yet (a form of debt.) When you receive an invoice you add it to the file, and then you remove it when you pay. Thus, the A/P is a form of credit that suppliers offer to their purchasers by allowing them to pay for a product or service after it has already been received.

a. Earnings before interest, taxes, depreciation and amortization
b. Accrual
c. Accounts receivable
d. Accounts payable

60. In economics, a _____ is a type of pension plan in which an employer promises a specified monthly benefit on retirement that is predetermined by a formula based on the employee's earnings history, tenure of service and age, rather than depending on investment returns. It is 'defined' in the sense that the formula for computing the employer's contribution is known in advance. In the United States, 26 U.S.C.

a. Fixed asset turnover
b. Defined benefit pension plan
c. 3M Company
d. BMC Software, Inc.

61. _____ and benefits in kind are various non-wage compensations provided to employees in addition to their normal wages or salaries. Where an employee exchanges (cash) wages for some other form of benefit, this is generally referred to as a 'salary sacrifice' arrangement. In most countries, most kinds of _____ are taxable to at least some degree.

a. AMEX
b. AIG
c. Employee benefits
d. ABC Television Network

62. In a company, _____ is the sum of all financial records of salaries, wages, bonuses and deductions.

A paycheck, is traditionally a paper document issued by an employer to pay an employee for services rendered. While most commonly used in the United States, recently the physical paycheck has been increasingly replaced by electronic direct deposit to bank accounts.

a. Total Expense Ratio
b. 3M Company
c. Tax expense
d. Payroll

Chapter 11. Reporting and Analyzing Equity

1. _____ is a concept whereby a person's financial liability is limited to a fixed sum, most commonly the value of a person's investment in a company or partnership with _____. A shareholder in a limited company is not personally liable for any of the debts of the company, other than for the value of his investment in that company. The same is true for the members of a _____ partnership and the limited partners in a limited partnership.
   a. Burden of proof
   b. Limited liability
   c. Joint venture
   d. Due diligence

2. _____ is the state or fact of exclusive rights and control over property, which may be an object, land/real estate or intellectual property. An _____ right is also referred to as title.

   _____ is the key building block in the development of the capitalist socio-economic system.

   a. Administrative proceeding
   b. Ownership
   c. ABC Television Network
   d. Encumbrance

3. The term _____ company refers to the ownership of a business company in two different ways: first, referring to ownership by non-governmental organizations; and second, referring to ownership of the company's stock by a relatively small number of holders who do not trade the stock publicly on the stock market. Less ambiguous terms for a _____ company are unquoted company and unlisted company.

   Though less visible than their publicly traded counterparts, private companies have a major importance in the world's economy.

   a. Privately held
   b. Freddie Mac
   c. Fannie Mae
   d. HFMA

4. A mutual shareholder or _____ is an individual or company (including a corporation) that legally owns one or more shares of stock in a joint stock company. A company's shareholders collectively own that company. Thus, the typical goal of such companies is to enhance shareholder value.
   a. Stockholder
   b. Growth investing
   c. 3M Company
   d. Stock split

5. In financial accounting, a _____ is defined as an obligation of an entity arising from past transactions or events, the settlement of which may result in the transfer or use of assets, provision of services or other yielding of economic benefits in the future.
   a. Liability
   b. False Claims Act
   c. Vested
   d. Corporate governance

6. A _____ is the pinnacle activity involved in selling products or services in return for money or other compensation. It is an act of completion of a commercial activity.

   A _____ is completed by the seller, the owner of the goods.

   a. High yield stock
   b. Sale
   c. Tertiary sector of economy
   d. Maturity

Chapter 11. Reporting and Analyzing Equity   113

7. A _____ is a body of elected or appointed members who jointly oversee the activities of a company or organization. The body sometimes has a different name, such as board of trustees, board of governors, board of managers, or executive board. It is often simply referred to as 'the board.'

A board's activities are determined by the powers, duties, and responsibilities delegated to it or conferred on it by an authority outside itself.

   a. Chief Financial Officers Act of 1990   b. Consumer protection laws
   c. Hospital Survey and Construction Act   d. Board of directors

8. _____ can refer to a law of local or limited application, passed under the authority of a higher law specifying what things may be regulated by the _____, or it can refer to the internal rules of a company or organisation.
   a. Scottish Poor Laws   b. Lease
   c. Letter of credit   d. Bylaw

9. In economics, _____ or _____ goods or real _____ refers to factors of production used to create goods or services that are not themselves significantly consumed (though they may depreciate) in the production process. _____ goods may be acquired with money or financial _____. In finance and accounting, _____ generally refers to financial wealth, especially that used to start or maintain a business.
   a. Vyborg Appeal   b. Disclosure
   c. Screening   d. Capital

10. In accounting, _____ has a very specific meaning. It is an outflow of cash or other valuable assets from a person or company to another person or company. This outflow of cash is generally one side of a trade for products or services that have equal or better current or future value to the buyer than to the seller.
   a. Expense   b. AIG
   c. AMEX   d. ABC Television Network

11. A _____ is a type of business entity in which partners (owners) share with each other the profits or losses of the business undertaking in which all have invested. _____s are often favored over corporations for taxation purposes, as the _____ structure does not generally incur a tax on profits before it is distributed to the partners (i.e. there is no dividend tax levied.) However, depending on the _____ structure and the jurisdiction in which it operates, owners of a _____ may be exposed to greater personal liability than they would as shareholders of a corporation.
   a. National Information Infrastructure Protection Act   b. Corporate governance
   c. Resource Conservation and Recovery Act   d. Partnership

12. _____ is any physical or virtual entity that is owned by an individual or jointly by a group of individuals. An owner of _____ has the right to consume, sell, rent, mortgage, transfer and exchange his or her _____. Important widely-recognized types of _____ include real _____, personal _____ (other physical possessions), and intellectual _____ (rights over artistic creations, inventions, etc.), although the latter is not always as widely recognized or enforced.
   a. Primary authority   b. Disclosure requirement
   c. Fiduciary   d. Property

13. _____, also known as property, plant, and equipment (PP&E), is a term used in accountancy for assets and property which cannot easily be converted into cash. This can be compared with current assets such as cash or bank accounts, which are described as liquid assets. In most cases, only tangible assets are referred to as fixed.

Chapter 11. Reporting and Analyzing Equity

    a. Subledger
    b. Bankruptcy prediction
    c. Fixed asset
    d. Minority interest

14. The _____ is a United States federal law that imposes a federal employer tax used to fund state workforce agencies. Employers report this tax by filing an annual Form 940 with the Internal Revenue Service.
    a. Council Tax
    b. Tax evasion
    c. Transfer tax
    d. Federal Unemployment Tax Act

15. A sole _____, or simply _____ is a type of business entity which legally has no separate existence from its owner. Hence, the limitations of liability enjoyed by a corporation and limited liability partnerships do not apply to sole proprietors. All debts of the business are debts of the owner.
    a. Proprietorship
    b. Pre-determined overhead rate
    c. Safety stock
    d. Free cash flow

16. A _____, or simply proprietorship is a type of business entity which legally has no separate existence from its owner. Hence, the limitations of liability enjoyed by a corporation and limited liability partnerships do not apply to sole proprietors. All debts of the business are debts of the owner.
    a. Time to market
    b. Customer satisfaction
    c. Free cash flow
    d. Sole proprietorship

17. A _____ or chief executive is one of the highest-ranking corporate officer (executive) or administrator in charge of total management. An individual selected as President and _____ of a corporation, company, organization, or agency, reports to the board of directors. In internal communication and press releases, many companies capitalize the term and those of other high positions, even when they are not proper nouns.
    a. Chief executive officer
    b. Kohlberg Kravis Roberts ' Co
    c. Return on equity
    d. Return on assets

18. _____ is a form of corporation equity ownership represented in the securities. It is a stock whose dividends are based on market fluctuations. It is dangerous in comparison to preferred shares and some other investment options, in that in the event of bankruptcy, _____ investors receive their funds after preferred stock holders, bondholders, creditors, etc. On the other hand, common shares on average perform better than preferred shares or bonds over time.
    a. Common stock
    b. 3M Company
    c. Growth investing
    d. Stock split

19. A _____ is a right to acquire certain property in preference to any other person. It usually refers to property newly coming into existence. A right to acquire existing property in preference to any other person is usually referred to as a right of first refusal.

In practice, the most common form of _____ is the right of existing shareholders to acquire newly issued shares issued by a company in a rights issue, a usually but not always public offering.

    a. Corporate governance
    b. Fiduciary
    c. Disclosure requirement
    d. Pre-emption right

20. In corporate law, a _____ is a legal document that certifies ownership of a specific number of stock shares in a corporation. In large corporations, buying shares does not always lead to a _____

Usually only shareholders with _____s can vote in a shareholders' general meeting.

a. BNSF Railway
c. 3M Company
b. Stock certificate
d. BMC Software, Inc.

21. Companies that have publicly traded securities typically use _____s to keep track of the individuals and entities that own their stocks and bonds. Most _____s are banks or trust companies, but sometimes a company acts as its own _____.

_____s perform three main functions:

1. Issue and cancel certificates to reflect changes in ownership. For example, when a company declares a stock dividend or stock split, the _____ issues new shares. _____s keep records of who owns a company's stocks and bonds and how those stocks and bonds are held--whether by the owner in certificate form, by the company in book-entry form, or by the investor's brokerage firm in street name. They also keep records of how many shares or bonds each investor owns.
2. Act as an intermediary for the company. A _____ may also serve as the company's paying agent to pay out interest, cash and stock dividends, or other distributions to stock- and bondholders. In addition, _____s act as proxy agent (sending out proxy materials), exchange agent (exchanging a company's stock or bonds in a merger), tender agent (tendering shares in a tender offer), and mailing agent (mailing the company's quarterly, annual, and other reports.)
3. Handle lost, destroyed, or stolen certificates. _____s help shareholders and bondholders when a stock or bond certificate has been lost, destroyed, or stolen.

In many cases, you can find out which _____ a company uses by visiting the investor relations section of the companye;s website.

a. Financial market
c. Mark-to-market
b. Market price
d. Transfer agent

22. _____, also referred to simply as a 'public offering' or 'flotation,' is when a company issues common stock or shares to the public for the first time. They are often issued by smaller, younger companies seeking capital to expand, but can also be done by large privately-owned companies looking to become publicly traded.

In an _____ the issuer may obtain the assistance of an underwriting firm, which helps it determine what type of security to issue (common or preferred), best offering price and time to bring it to market.

a. Initial public offering
c. AT'T Wireless Services, Inc.
b. Intergenerational equity
d. Insolvency

Chapter 11. Reporting and Analyzing Equity

23. A _____ has several related meanings:

   - a daily record of events or business; a private _____ is usually referred to as a diary.
   - a newspaper or other periodical, in the literal sense of one published each day;
   - many publications issued at stated intervals, such as magazines, or scholarly academic _____s, or the record of the transactions of a society, are often called _____s. Although _____ is sometimes used, erroneously, as a synonym for 'magazine,' in academic use, a _____ refers to a serious, scholarly publication, most often peer-reviewed. A non-scholarly magazine written for an educated audience about an industry or an area of professional activity is usually called a professional magazine.

The word 'journalist' for one whose business is writing for the public press has been in use since the end of the 17th century.

Open access _____s are scholarly _____s that are available to the reader without financial or other barrier other than access to the internet itself. Some are subsidized, and some require payment on behalf of the author. Subsidized _____s are financed by an academic institution or a government information center.

   a. 3M Company
   c. BMC Software, Inc.
   b. BNSF Railway
   d. Journal

24. A _____ is any one of a variety of different systems, institutions, procedures, social relations and infrastructures whereby persons trade, and goods and services are exchanged, forming part of the economy. It is an arrangement that allows buyers and sellers to exchange things. _____s vary in size, range, geographic scale, location, types and variety of human communities, as well as the types of goods and services traded.
   a. Market
   c. Perfect competition
   b. Recession
   d. Market Failure

25. _____ is the price at which an asset would trade in a competitive Walrasian auction setting. _____ is often used interchangeably with open _____, fair value or fair _____, although these terms have distinct definitions in different standards, and may differ in some circumstances.

International Valuation Standards defines _____ as 'the estimated amount for which a property should exchange on the date of valuation between a willing buyer and a willing seller in an arme;s-length transaction after proper marketing wherein the parties had each acted knowledgeably, prudently, and without compulsion.'

_____ is a concept distinct from market price, which is e;the price at which one can transacte;, while _____ is e;the true underlying valuee; according to theoretical standards.

   a. Market value
   c. Debtor
   b. Sinking fund
   d. Segregated portfolio company

26. _____ are common shares that have been authorized, issued, and purchased by investors. They have voting rights and represent ownership in the corporation by the person or institution that holds the shares. They should be distinguished from treasury shares, which are common stock repurchased by the corporation.

a. Controlling interest
c. Preferred stock
b. Participating preferred stock
d. Shares outstanding

27. _____, in finance and accounting, means stated value or face value. From this comes the expressions at par (at the _____), over par (over _____) and under par (under _____).

_____ is a nominal value of a security which is determined by an issuer company at a minimum price. _____ of an equity (a stock) is a somewhat archaic concept. The _____ of a stock was the share price upon initial offering; the issuing company promised not to issue further shares below _____, so investors could be confident that no one else was receiving a more favorable issue price. This was far more important in unregulated equity markets than in the regulated markets that exist today.

a. Creditor
c. Restructuring
b. Net worth
d. Par value

28. Initial _____, also referred to simply as a '_____' or 'flotation,' is when a company issues common stock or shares to the public for the first time. They are often issued by smaller, younger companies seeking capital to expand, but can also be done by large privately-owned companies looking to become publicly traded.

In an Ipublic offering the issuer may obtain the assistance of an underwriting firm, which helps it determine what type of security to issue (common or preferred), best offering price and time to bring it to market.

a. Restricted stock
c. Gross income
b. Commercial paper
d. Public offering

29. _____ is a specific term used in companies' financial reporting from the company-whole point of view. Because that use excludes the effects of changing ownership interest, an economic measure of _____ is necessary for financial analysis from the shareholders' point of view

_____ is defined by the Financial Accounting Standards Board, or FASB, as 'the change in equity [net assets] of a business enterprise during a period from transactions and other events and circumstances from nonowner sources. It includes all changes in equity during a period except those resulting from investments by owners and distributions to owners.'

_____ is the sum of net income and other items that must bypass the income statement because they have not been realized, including items like an unrealized holding gain or loss from available for sale securities and foreign currency translation gains or losses.

a. BMC Software, Inc.
c. BNSF Railway
b. 3M Company
d. Comprehensive income

30. Discounting is a financial mechanism in which a debtor obtains the right to delay payments to a creditor, for a defined period of time, in exchange for a charge or fee. Essentially, the party that owes money in the present purchases the right to delay the payment until some future date. The _____, or charge, is simply the difference between the original amount owed in the present and the amount that has to be paid in the future to settle the debt.

a. Risk aversion
b. Discount factor
c. Discount
d. Discounting

31. In business and accounting, _____ are everything of value that is owned by a person or company. It is a claim on the property your income of a borrower. The balance sheet of a firm records the monetary value of the _____ owned by the firm.
   a. Accounts receivable
   b. Accrual basis accounting
   c. Earnings before interest, taxes, depreciation and amortization
   d. Assets

32. _____ and credit are formal bookkeeping and accounting terms. They are the most fundamental concepts in accounting, representing the two records that one party in a transaction makes on its records, transferring a money balance from one account to another, one representing a reduction of liability or increase in asset, and the other representing a balancing increase in liability or reduction of asset.

Introduction

_____s and credits are a system of notation used in accounting to keep track of money movements (transactions) into and out of an account.

   a. Debit and credit
   b. Bookkeeping
   c. Debit
   d. Cookie jar accounting

33. _____ are payments made by a corporation to its shareholder members. It is the portion of corporate profits paid out to stockholders. When a corporation earns a profit or surplus, that money can be put to two uses: it can either be re-invested in the business (called retained earnings), or it can be paid to the shareholders as a dividend.
   a. Dividend yield
   b. Dividend stripping
   c. Dividend payout ratio
   d. Dividends

34. A budget _____ occurs when an entity spends more money than it takes in. The opposite of a budget _____ is a budget surplus. Debt is essentially an accumulated flow of _____s.
   a. Deficit
   b. Land value taxation
   c. Windfall profits tax
   d. Progressive tax

35. A _____ is the transfer of wealth from one party (such as a person or company) to another. A _____ is usually made in exchange for the provision of goods, services or both, or to fulfill a legal obligation.

The simplest and oldest form of _____ is barter, the exchange of one good or service for another.

   a. 3M Company
   b. Payee
   c. BMC Software, Inc.
   d. Payment

36. _____ is a payment of a dividend to stockholders that exceeds the company's retained earnings. Once retained earnings is depleted, capital accounts such as additional paid-in capital are decreased to make up for the remaining dividend to be paid to stockholders. When a _____ occurs, it is considered to be a return of investment instead of profits.

Chapter 11. Reporting and Analyzing Equity

a. Liquidating dividend
b. Redemption value
c. Trade name
d. Fund accounting

37. _____ is typically a 'higher ranking' stock than voting shares, and its terms are negotiated between the corporation and the investor.

_____ usually carries no voting rights, but may carry superior priority over common stock in the payment of dividends and upon liquidation. _____ may carry a dividend that is paid out prior to any dividends being paid to common stock holders.

a. Restricted stock
b. Gross income
c. Cash flow
d. Preferred stock

38. On a stock exchange, a _____ or reverse split is the opposite of a stock split, i.e. a stock merge - a reduction in the number of shares and an accompanying increase in the share price. The ratio is also reversed: 1-for-2, 1-for-3 and so on.

There is a stigma attached to doing this so it is not initiated without very good reason.

a. Reverse stock split
b. Discount rate
c. Cost of capital
d. Public good

39. A _____ or stock divide increases or decreases the number of shares in a public company. The price is adjusted such that the before and after market capitalization of the company remains the same and dilution does not occur. Options and warrants are included.

a. Growth investing
b. 3M Company
c. Stockholder
d. Stock split

40. _____ is a legal term for a type of debt which is overdue after missing an expected payment. It is also used (in the form in _____) for payments that occur at the end of a period.

_____ accrue from the date on the first missed payment was due. The term is often used to describe being late with rent, bills, royalties (or other contractual payments), child support, or other legal financial obligation.

a. AIG
b. ABC Television Network
c. Interest
d. Arrears

41. _____ is capital stock which provides a specific dividend that is paid before any dividends are paid to common stock holders, and which takes precedence over common stock in the event of a liquidation. This form of financing is used by private equity investors and venture capital firms. Holders of _____ get both their money back (with interest) and the money that is distributable with respect to the percentage of common shares into which their preferred stock can convert.

a. Commercial paper
b. Cash flow
c. Participating preferred stock
d. Gross income

Chapter 11. Reporting and Analyzing Equity

42. The _____ of 2002 (Pub.L. 107-204, 116 Stat. 745, enacted July 30, 2002), also known as the Public Company Accounting Reform and Investor Protection Act of 2002, is a United States federal law enacted on July 30, 2002 in response to a number of major corporate and accounting scandals including those affecting Enron, Tyco International, Adelphia, Peregrine Systems and WorldCom. The legislation establishes new or enhanced standards for all U.S. public company boards, management, and public accounting firms. It does not apply to privately held companies.
    a. Fair Labor Standards Act
    b. Sarbanes-Oxley Act
    c. Lease
    d. FCPA

43. A _____ is a type of bond that allows the issuer of the bond to retain the privilege of redeeming the bond at some point before the bond reaches the date of maturity. In other words, on the call dates, the issuer has the right, but not the obligation, to buy back the bonds from the bond holders at the call price. Technically speaking, the bonds are not really bought and held by the issuer but cancelled immediately.
    a. Callable bond
    b. Coupon rate
    c. Catastrophe bonds
    d. Zero-coupon

44. In finance, a _____ is a type of bond that can be converted into shares of stock in the issuing company, usually at some pre-announced ratio. It is a hybrid security with debt- and equity-like features. Although it typically has a low coupon rate, the holder is compensated with the ability to convert the bond to common stock, usually at a substantial discount to the stock's market value.
    a. Convertible bond
    b. Zero-coupon
    c. Zero-coupon bond
    d. Coupon rate

45. _____ is the price at which the issuing company may choose to repurchase a security before its maturity date.

A bond is purchased at a discount if its _____ exceeds its purchase price. It is purchased at a premium if its purchase price exceeds its _____.

    a. Consolidated financial statements
    b. Trade name
    c. Lump sum
    d. Redemption value

46. _____ measures the rate of return on the ownership interest (shareholders' equity) of the common stock owners. It measures a firm's efficiency at generating profits from every dollar of shareholders' equity (also known as net assets or assets minus liabilities.) It shows how well a company uses investment dollars to generate earnings growth.
    a. Return on equity
    b. Return on capital employed
    c. Sortino ratio
    d. Like for like

47. _____ in economics and business is the result of an exchange and from that trade we assign a numerical monetary value to a good, service or asset. If Alice trades Bob 4 apples for an orange, the _____ of an orange is 4 apples. Inversely, the _____ of an apple is 1/4 oranges.
    a. Price
    b. Price discrimination
    c. Transactional Net Margin Method
    d. Discounts and allowances

48. In economics, business, retail, and accounting, a _____ is the value of money that has been used up to produce something, and hence is not available for use anymore. In economics, a _____ is an alternative that is given up as a result of a decision. In business, the _____ may be one of acquisition, in which case the amount of money expended to acquire it is counted as _____.

Chapter 11. Reporting and Analyzing Equity

a. Cost of quality
b. Prime cost
c. Cost allocation
d. Cost

49. A _____ or reacquired stock is stock which is bought back by the issuing company, reducing the amount of outstanding stock on the open market ('open market' including insiders' holdings).

Stock repurchases are often used as a tax-efficient method to put cash into shareholders' hands, rather than pay dividends. Sometimes, companies do this when they feel that their stock is undervalued on the open market.

a. Treasury stock
b. Net profit
c. Matching principle
d. Cost of goods sold

50. _____ refers to a business or organization attempting to acquire goods or services to accomplish the goals of the enterprise. Though there are several organizations that attempt to set standards in the _____ process, processes can vary greatly between organizations. Typically the word e;_____e; is not used interchangeably with the word e;procuremente;, since procurement typically includes Expediting, Supplier Quality, and Traffic and Logistics (T'L) in addition to _____.

a. Supply chain
b. Free port
c. Consignor
d. Purchasing

51. _____ are formal bookkeeping and accounting terms. They are the most fundamental concepts in accounting, representing the two records that one party in a transaction makes on its records, transferring a money balance from one account to another, one representing a reduction of liability or increase in asset, and the other representing a balancing increase in liability or reduction of asset.

Debits and credits are a system of notation used in accounting to keep track of money movements (transactions) into and out of an account.

a. Bookkeeping
b. Cookie jar accounting
c. Controlling account
d. Debit and credit

52. An _____ is a period with reference to which United Kingdom corporation tax is charged. It helps dictate when tax is paid on income and gains. An _____ begins whenever a company comes within the corporation tax charge, and whenever an _____ ends without the company ceasing to be within the charge.

a. Accounting period
b. AIG
c. ABC Television Network
d. AMEX

Chapter 11. Reporting and Analyzing Equity

53. _____ is the act of taking possession of or assigning purpose to properties or ideas and is important in many topics, including:

- _____ in relation to the spread of knowledge
- _____ (art)
  - _____ (music) in reference to the re-use and proliferation of different types of music
- _____ (economics) origination of human ownership of previously unowned natural resources such as land
- _____ (law) as a component of government spending
- Cultural _____ is the borrowing, or theft, of an element of cultural expression of one group by another.
- The tort of _____ is one form of invasion of privacy.

a. Intangible
c. Annuity
b. Improvement
d. Appropriation

54. The _____ is one of the basic financial statements as per Generally Accepted Accounting Principles, and it explains the changes in a company's retained earnings over the reporting period. It breaks down changes affecting the account, such as profits or losses from operations, dividends paid, and any other items charged or credited to retained earnings. A retained earnings statement is required by Generally Accepted Accounting Principles whenever comparative balance sheets and income statements are presented.

a. 3M Company
c. Financial statements
b. Statement of retained earnings
d. Notes to the financial statements

55. In accounting/accountancy, _____ are journal entries usually made at the end of an accounting period to allocate income and expenditure to the period in which they actually occurred. The revenue recognition principle is the basis of making _____ that pertain to unearned and accrued revenues under accrual-basis accounting. They are sometimes called Balance Day adjustments because they are made on balance day.

a. Accrual
c. Adjusting entries
b. Accrued expense
d. Earnings before interest, taxes, depreciation and amortization

56. In finance, an _____ is a contract between a buyer and a seller that gives the buyer the right--but not the obligation--to buy or to sell a particular asset (the underlying asset) at a later time at an agreed price. In return for granting the _____, the seller collects a payment (the premium) from the buyer. A call _____ gives the buyer the right to buy the underlying asset; a put _____ gives the buyer of the _____ the right to sell the underlying asset.

a. Option
c. AMEX
b. ABC Television Network
d. AIG

57. _____ are the earnings returned on the initial investment amount.

In the US, the Financial Accounting Standards Board (FASB) requires companies' income statements to report _____ for each of the major categories of the income statement: continuing operations, discontinued operations, extraordinary items, and net income.

The _____ formula does not include preferred dividends for categories outside of continued operations and net income.

Chapter 11. Reporting and Analyzing Equity

a. Earnings yield
c. Invested capital

b. Average accounting return
d. Earnings per share

58. _____ is equal to the income that a firm has after subtracting costs and expenses from the total revenue. _____ can be distributed among holders of common stock as a dividend or held by the firm as retained earnings.

The items deducted will typically include tax expense, financing expense (interest expense), and minority interest. Likewise, preferred stock dividends will be subtracted too, though they are not an expense.

a. Long-term liabilities
c. Matching principle

b. Generally accepted accounting principles
d. Net income

59. _____ is the balance of the amounts of cash being received and paid by a business during a defined period of time, sometimes tied to a specific project. Measurement of _____ can be used

- to evaluate the state or performance of a business or project.
- to determine problems with liquidity. Being profitable does not necessarily mean being liquid. A company can fail because of a shortage of cash, even while profitable.
- to project rate of returns. The time of _____s into and out of projects are used as inputs to financial models such as internal rate of return, and net present value.
- to examine income or growth of a business when it is believed that accrual accounting concepts do not represent economic realities. Alternately, _____ can be used to 'validate' the net income generated by accrual accounting.

_____ as a generic term may be used differently depending on context, and certain _____ definitions may be adapted by analysts and users for their own uses. Common terms include operating _____ and free _____.

a. Cash flow
c. Commercial paper

b. Controlling interest
d. Flow-through entity

60. The _____ on a company stock is the company's annual dividend payments divided by its market cap, or the dividend per share divided by the price per share. It is often expressed as a percentage.

Dividend payments on preferred shares are stipulated by the prospectus.

a. Dividend stripping
c. Dividends

b. Dividend payout ratio
d. Dividend yield

61. In finance, the term _____ describes the amount in cash that returns to the owners of a security. Normally it does not include the price variations, at the difference of the total return. _____ applies to various stated rates of return on stocks (common and preferred, and convertible), fixed income instruments (bonds, notes, bills, strips, zero coupon), and some other investment type insurance products (e.g. annuities.)

a. Disclosure
c. Yield

b. Residence trusts
d. Pension System

62. In accounting, _____ or carrying value is the value of an asset according to its balance sheet account balance. For assets, the value is based on the original cost of the asset less any depreciation, amortization or impairment costs made against the asset. Traditionally, a company's _____ is its total assets minus intangible assets and liabilities.
   a. Matching principle
   b. Generally accepted accounting principles
   c. Book value
   d. Depreciation

63. _____ is the fraction of net income a firm pays to its stockholders in dividends:

The part of the earnings not paid to investors is left for investment to provide for future earnings growth. Investors seeking high current income and limited capital growth prefer companies with high _____. However investors seeking capital growth may prefer lower payout ratio because capital gains are taxed at a lower rate.

   a. Dividends
   b. Dividend yield
   c. Dividend stripping
   d. Dividend payout ratio

Chapter 12. Reporting and Analyzing Cash Flows

1. _____ is the balance of the amounts of cash being received and paid by a business during a defined period of time, sometimes tied to a specific project. Measurement of _____ can be used

   - to evaluate the state or performance of a business or project.
   - to determine problems with liquidity. Being profitable does not necessarily mean being liquid. A company can fail because of a shortage of cash, even while profitable.
   - to project rate of returns. The time of _____s into and out of projects are used as inputs to financial models such as internal rate of return, and net present value.
   - to examine income or growth of a business when it is believed that accrual accounting concepts do not represent economic realities. Alternately, _____ can be used to 'validate' the net income generated by accrual accounting.

   _____ as a generic term may be used differently depending on context, and certain _____ definitions may be adapted by analysts and users for their own uses. Common terms include operating _____ and free _____.

   a. Flow-through entity
   b. Cash flow
   c. Controlling interest
   d. Commercial paper

2. An _____ is a term used in behavioral economics to describe those types of behaviors that impose costs on a person in the long-run that are not taken into account when making decisions in the present. Classical Economics discourages government from creating legislation that targets internalities, because it is assumed that the consumer takes these personal costs into account when paying for the good that causes the _____. For example, cigarettes should be taxed because of the negative consumption externalities that they impose, such as second-hand smoke, not because the smoker harms him or herself by smoking.
   a. Authorised capital
   b. Operating budget
   c. Inventory turnover ratio
   d. Internality

3. In financial accounting, a _____ or Statement of cash flows is a financial statement that shows a company's flow of cash. The money coming into the business is called cash inflow, and money going out from the business is called cash outflow. The statement shows how changes in balance sheet and income accounts affect cash and cash equivalents, and breaks the analysis down to operating, investing, and financing activities.
   a. BNSF Railway
   b. BMC Software, Inc.
   c. 3M Company
   d. Cash flow statement

4. _____ are the most liquid assets found within the asset portion of a company's balance sheet. Cash equivalents are assets that are readily convertible into cash, such as money market holdings, short-term government bonds or Treasury bills, marketable securities and commercial paper. _____ are distinguished from other investments through their short-term existence; they mature within 3 months whereas short-term investments are 12 months or less, and long-term investments are any investments that mature in excess of 12 months.
   a. Cash and cash equivalents
   b. Par value
   c. Debtor
   d. Payback period

5. A loan is a type of debt. Like all debt instruments, a loan entails the redistribution of financial assets over time, between the _____ and the borrower.

   In a loan, the borrower initially receives or borrows an amount of money, called the principal, from the _____, and is obligated to pay back or repay an equal amount of money to the _____ at a later time.

Chapter 12. Reporting and Analyzing Cash Flows

    a. Loan to value
    b. Debt
    c. Credit rating
    d. Lender

6. In financial accounting, _____ , cash flow provided by operations or cash flow from operating activities, refers to the amount of cash a company generates from the revenues it brings in, excluding costs associated with long-term investment on capital items or investment in securities.

_____ = Cash generated from operations less taxation and interest paid, investment income received and less dividends paid gives rise to _____s per International Financial Reporting Standards.

To calculate cash generated from operations, one must calculate cash generated from customers and cash paid to suppliers.

    a. ABC Television Network
    b. Operating cash flow
    c. AMEX
    d. AIG

7. In finance, _____ is the process of estimating the potential market value of a financial asset or liability. They can be done on assets (for example, investments in marketable securities such as stocks, options, business enterprises, or intangible assets such as patents and trademarks) or on liabilities (e.g., Bonds issued by a company.) A _____ is required in many contexts including investment analysis, capital budgeting, merger and acquisition transactions, financial reporting, taxable events to determine the proper tax liability, and in litigation.
    a. Disclosure
    b. Daybook
    c. Valuation
    d. Vyborg Appeal

8. The _____ is a private, not-for-profit organization whose primary purpose is to develop generally accepted accounting principles (GAAP) within the United States in the public's interest. The Securities and Exchange Commission (SEC) designated the _____ as the organization responsible for setting accounting standards for public companies in the U.S. It was created in 1973, replacing the Accounting Principles Board and the Committee on Accounting Procedure of the American Institute of Certified Public Accountants. The _____'s mission is 'to establish and improve standards of financial accounting and reporting for the guidance and education of the public, including issuers, auditors, and users of financial information.'

The _____ is not a governmental body.

    a. Fannie Mae
    b. Governmental Accounting Standards Board
    c. Financial Accounting Standards Board
    d. Public company

9. In economic models, the _____ time frame assumes no fixed factors of production. Firms can enter or leave the marketplace, and the cost (and availability) of land, labor, raw materials, and capital goods can be assumed to vary. In contrast, in the short-run time frame, certain factors are assumed to be fixed, because there is not sufficient time for them to change.
    a. Long-run
    b. 3M Company
    c. Short-run
    d. BMC Software, Inc.

10. _____ are liabilities with a future benefit over one year, such as notes payable that mature greater than one year.

In accounting, the _____ are shown on the right wing of the balance-sheet representing the sources of funds, which are generally bounded in form of capital assets.

Examples of _____ are debentures, mortgage loans and other bank loans (note: not all bank loans are long term as not all are paid over a period greater than a year, the example is bridging loan.)

a. Gross sales
c. Cash basis accounting
b. Book value
d. Long-term liabilities

11. The _____ of 2002 (Pub.L. 107-204, 116 Stat. 745, enacted July 30, 2002), also known as the Public Company Accounting Reform and Investor Protection Act of 2002, is a United States federal law enacted on July 30, 2002 in response to a number of major corporate and accounting scandals including those affecting Enron, Tyco International, Adelphia, Peregrine Systems and WorldCom. The legislation establishes new or enhanced standards for all U.S. public company boards, management, and public accounting firms. It does not apply to privately held companies.
a. Lease
c. Fair Labor Standards Act
b. Sarbanes-Oxley Act
d. FCPA

12. In business and accounting, _____ are everything of value that is owned by a person or company. It is a claim on the property your income of a borrower. The balance sheet of a firm records the monetary value of the _____ owned by the firm.
a. Earnings before interest, taxes, depreciation and amortization
c. Accrual basis accounting
b. Accounts receivable
d. Assets

13. In financial accounting, a _____ is defined as an obligation of an entity arising from past transactions or events, the settlement of which may result in the transfer or use of assets, provision of services or other yielding of economic benefits in the future.
a. Vested
c. Corporate governance
b. False Claims Act
d. Liability

14. _____ are payments made by a corporation to its shareholder members. It is the portion of corporate profits paid out to stockholders. When a corporation earns a profit or surplus, that money can be put to two uses: it can either be re-invested in the business (called retained earnings), or it can be paid to the shareholders as a dividend.
a. Dividend stripping
c. Dividend payout ratio
b. Dividend yield
d. Dividends

15. An account statement or a _____ is a summary of all financial transactions occurring over a given period of time on a deposit account, a credit card, or any other type of account offered by a financial institution.

_____s are typically printed on one or several pieces of paper and either mailed directly to the account holder's address, or kept at the financial institution's local branch for pick-up. Certain ATMs offer the possibility to print, at any time, a condensed version of a _____.

a. 3M Company
b. BMC Software, Inc.
c. Bank statement
d. BNSF Railway

16. _____ is application software that records and processes accounting transactions within functional modules such as accounts payable, accounts receivable, payroll, and trial balance. It functions as an accounting information system. It may be developed in-house by the company or organization using it, may be purchased from a third party, or may be a combination of a third-party application software package with local modifications.
   a. Accounting software
   b. Economic value added
   c. AIG
   d. Amgen

17. In finance, a _____ is a debt security, in which the authorized issuer owes the holders a debt and, depending on the terms of the _____, is obliged to pay interest (the coupon) and/or to repay the principal at a later date, termed maturity. It is a formal contract to repay borrowed money with interest at fixed intervals.

Thus a _____ is like a loan: the issuer is the borrower, the _____ holder is the lender, and the coupon is the interest.

   a. Bond
   b. Revenue bonds
   c. Coupon rate
   d. Zero-coupon bond

18. In economics, _____ or _____ goods or real _____ refers to factors of production used to create goods or services that are not themselves significantly consumed (though they may depreciate) in the production process. _____ goods may be acquired with money or financial _____. In finance and accounting, _____ generally refers to financial wealth, especially that used to start or maintain a business.
   a. Disclosure
   b. Capital
   c. Vyborg Appeal
   d. Screening

19. A _____, also client, buyer or purchaser is the buyer or user of the paid products of an individual or organization, mostly called the supplier or seller. This is typically through purchasing or renting goods or services.
   a. Customer
   b. BNSF Railway
   c. 3M Company
   d. BMC Software, Inc.

20. An _____ is a tax levied on the financial income of people, corporations, or other legal entities. Various _____ systems exist, with varying degrees of tax incidence. Income taxation can be progressive, proportional, or regressive.
   a. Implied level of government service
   b. Individual Retirement Arrangement
   c. Ordinary income
   d. Income tax

21. _____ is a fee paid on borrowed assets. It is the price paid for the use of borrowed money, or, money earned by deposited funds. Assets that are sometimes lent with _____ include money, shares, consumer goods through hire purchase, major assets such as aircraft, and even entire factories in finance lease arrangements. The _____ is calculated upon the value of the assets in the same manner as upon money.
   a. AIG
   b. ABC Television Network
   c. Insolvency
   d. Interest

Chapter 12. Reporting and Analyzing Cash Flows

22. A _____ is the transfer of wealth from one party (such as a person or company) to another. A _____ is usually made in exchange for the provision of goods, services or both, or to fulfill a legal obligation.

The simplest and oldest form of _____ is barter, the exchange of one good or service for another.

a. 3M Company
c. Payee
b. BMC Software, Inc.
d. Payment

23. _____ is a financial metric which represents operating liquidity available to a business. Along with fixed assets such as plant and equipment, _____ is considered a part of operating capital. It is calculated as current assets minus current liabilities.

a. Working capital management
c. 3M Company
b. BMC Software, Inc.
d. Working capital

24. The basic _____ is the foundation for the double-entry bookkeeping system. It shows how assets were financed: either by borrowing money from someone (liability) or by paying your own money (shareholders' equity.)

Assets = Liabilities + (Shareholders or Owners equity)

For example: A student buys a computer for $945.

a. AMEX
c. Accounting equation
b. ABC Television Network
d. AIG

25. An _____ is a period with reference to which United Kingdom corporation tax is charged. It helps dictate when tax is paid on income and gains. An _____ begins whenever a company comes within the corporation tax charge, and whenever an _____ ends without the company ceasing to be within the charge.

a. AMEX
c. AIG
b. ABC Television Network
d. Accounting period

26. _____ is a file or account that contains money that a person or company owes to suppliers, but has not paid yet (a form of debt.) When you receive an invoice you add it to the file, and then you remove it when you pay. Thus, the A/P is a form of credit that suppliers offer to their purchasers by allowing them to pay for a product or service after it has already been received.

a. Accounts receivable
b. Earnings before interest, taxes, depreciation and amortization
c. Accounts payable
d. Accrual

27. _____ is one of a series of accounting transactions dealing with the billing of customers who owe money to a person, company or organization for goods and services that have been provided to the customer. In most business entities this is typically done by generating an invoice and mailing or electronically delivering it to the customer, who in turn must pay it within an established timeframe called credit or payment terms.

An example of a common payment term is Net 30, meaning payment is due in the amount of the invoice 30 days from the date of invoice.

a. Accrued revenue
c. Accrual
b. Adjusting entries
d. Accounts receivable

28. _____ is a specific term used in companies' financial reporting from the company-whole point of view. Because that use excludes the effects of changing ownership interest, an economic measure of _____ is necessary for financial analysis from the shareholders' point of view

_____ is defined by the Financial Accounting Standards Board, or FASB, as 'the change in equity [net assets] of a business enterprise during a period from transactions and other events and circumstances from nonowner sources. It includes all changes in equity during a period except those resulting from investments by owners and distributions to owners.'

_____ is the sum of net income and other items that must bypass the income statement because they have not been realized, including items like an unrealized holding gain or loss from available for sale securities and foreign currency translation gains or losses.

a. Comprehensive income
c. BNSF Railway
b. 3M Company
d. BMC Software, Inc.

29. A _____ is a fungible, negotiable instrument representing financial value. they are broadly categorized into debt securities (such as banknotes, bonds and debentures), and equity securities; e.g., common stocks. The company or other entity issuing the _____ is called the issuer.

a. Tracking stock
c. 3M Company
b. BMC Software, Inc.
d. Security

30. In financial accounting, a _____ or statement of financial position is a summary of a person's or organization's balances. Assets, liabilities and ownership equity are listed as of a specific date, such as the end of its financial year. A _____ is often described as a snapshot of a company's financial condition.

a. 3M Company
c. Statement of retained earnings
b. Balance sheet
d. Financial statements

31. _____ is a company's financial statement that indicates how the revenue is transformed into the net income The purpose of the _____ is to show managers and investors whether the company made or lost money during the period being reported.

The important thing to remember about an _____ is that it represents a period of time.

a. AMEX
c. AIG
b. ABC Television Network
d. Income statement

32. _____ are formal records of a business' financial activities.

In British English, including United Kingdom company law, _____ are often referred to as accounts, although the term _____ is also used, particularly by accountants.

_____ provide an overview of a business' financial condition in both short and long term.

Chapter 12. Reporting and Analyzing Cash Flows

a. Notes to the financial statements
c. 3M Company
b. Statement of retained earnings
d. Financial statements

33. A _____ is a compensation, usually financial, received by a worker in exchange for their labor.

Compensation in terms of _____s is given to worker and compensation in terms of salary is given to employees. Compensation is a monetary benefits given to employees in returns of the services provided by them.

a. Retirement plan
c. BMC Software, Inc.
b. 3M Company
d. Wage

34. In accounting, a _____ is an asset on the balance sheet which is expected to be sold or otherwise used up in the near future, usually within one year, or one business cycle - whichever is longer. Typical _____s include cash, cash equivalents, accounts receivable, inventory, the portion of prepaid accounts which will be used within a year, and short-term investments.

On the balance sheet, assets will typically be classified into _____s and long-term assets.

a. Current asset
c. Deferred
b. General ledger
d. Pro forma

35. In accounting, _____ has a very specific meaning. It is an outflow of cash or other valuable assets from a person or company to another person or company. This outflow of cash is generally one side of a trade for products or services that have equal or better current or future value to the buyer than to the seller.

a. AIG
c. ABC Television Network
b. AMEX
d. Expense

36. _____ is equal to the income that a firm has after subtracting costs and expenses from the total revenue. _____ can be distributed among holders of common stock as a dividend or held by the firm as retained earnings.

The items deducted will typically include tax expense, financing expense (interest expense), and minority interest. Likewise, preferred stock dividends will be subtracted too, though they are not an expense.

a. Long-term liabilities
c. Matching principle
b. Generally accepted accounting principles
d. Net income

37. An _____, operating expenditure, operational expense, operational expenditure or OPEX is an on-going cost for running a product, business, or system. Its counterpart, a capital expenditure (CAPEX), is the cost of developing or providing non-consumable parts for the product or system. For example, the purchase of a photocopier is the CAPEX, and the annual paper and toner cost is the OPEX.

a. AMEX
c. ABC Television Network
b. Operating expense
d. AIG

Chapter 12. Reporting and Analyzing Cash Flows

38. A _____ is a computer application that simulates a paper worksheet. It displays multiple cells that together make up a grid consisting of rows and columns, each cell containing either alphanumeric text or numeric values. A _____ cell may alternatively contain a formula that defines how the contents of that cell is to be calculated from the contents of any other cell (or combination of cells) each time any cell is updated.

    a. Linear regression
    c. Merck ' Co., Inc.
    b. Spreadsheet
    d. Mutual fund

39. _____ are liabilities which have occurred, but have not been paid or logged under accounts payable during an accounting period; in other words, obligations for goods and services provided to a company for which invoices have not yet been received. Examples would include accrued wages payable, accrued sales tax payable, and accrued rent payable.

There are two general types of _____:

- Routine and recurring
- Infrequent or non-routine

Most companies pay their employees on a predetermined schedule. Let's say that the 'Imaginary company Ltd.' pays its employees each Friday for the hours worked that week.

    a. ABC Television Network
    c. AIG
    b. Accrued Liabilities
    d. AMEX

40. _____ is the process of matching and comparing figures from accounting records against those presented on a bank statement. Less any items which have no relation to the bank statement, the balance of the accounting ledger should reconcile (match) to the balance of the bank statement.

_____ allows companies or individuals to compare their account records to the bank's records of their account balance in order to uncover any possible discrepancies.

    a. Lower of Cost or Market
    c. Bank reconciliation
    b. Credit memo
    d. Bankruptcy prediction

41. _____ refers to services paid for in advance. Examples include tolls, pay as you go cell phones, and stored-value cards such as gift cards and preloaded credit cards. _____ accounts are assets, and they are increased by debiting the account(s.)

    a. BMC Software, Inc.
    c. BNSF Railway
    b. 3M Company
    d. Prepaid

42. _____, in accrual accounting, is any account where the asset or liability is not realized until a future date (accounting period), e.g. annuities, charges, taxes, income, etc. The _____ item may be carried, dependent on type of deferral, as either an asset or liability.

    a. Payroll
    c. Deferred
    b. Pro forma
    d. Cash basis accounting

43. In accounting, _____ are considered liabilities of the business that are to be settled in cash within the fiscal year or the operating cycle, whichever period is longer.

For example accounts payable for goods, services or supplies that were purchased for use in the operation of the business and payable within a normal period of time would be _____.

Bonds, mortgages and loans that are payable over a term exceeding one year would be fixed liabilities.

a. Current liabilities
b. Payroll
c. Treasury stock
d. Closing entries

44. _____ is a term used in accounting, economics and finance to spread the cost of an asset over the span of several years.

In simple words we can say that _____ is the reduction in the value of an asset due to usage, passage of time, wear and tear, technological outdating or obsolescence, depletion, inadequacy, rot, rust, decay or other such factors.

In accounting, _____ is a term used to describe any method of attributing the historical or purchase cost of an asset across its useful life, roughly corresponding to normal wear and tear.

a. General ledger
b. Depreciation
c. Current asset
d. Net profit

45. _____ is that which is owed; usually referencing assets owed, but the term can also cover moral obligations and other interactions not requiring money. In the case of assets, _____ is a means of using future purchasing power in the present before a summation has been earned. Some companies and corporations use _____ as a part of their overall corporate finance strategy.

a. Debt
b. Lender
c. Loan
d. Debenture

46. _____ is the term used to refer to the standard framework of guidelines for financial accounting used in any given jurisdiction. _____ includes the standards, conventions, and rules accountants follow in recording and summarizing transactions, and in the preparation of financial statements.

Financial accounting information must be assembled and reported objectively.

a. Current asset
b. General ledger
c. Long-term liabilities
d. Generally accepted accounting principles

47. A _____ is the pinnacle activity involved in selling products or services in return for money or other compensation. It is an act of completion of a commercial activity.

A _____ is completed by the seller, the owner of the goods.

Chapter 12. Reporting and Analyzing Cash Flows

a. Maturity
b. Tertiary sector of economy
c. High yield stock
d. Sale

48. _____ is a form of corporation equity ownership represented in the securities. It is a stock whose dividends are based on market fluctuations. It is dangerous in comparison to preferred shares and some other investment options, in that in the event of bankruptcy, _____ investors receive their funds after preferred stock holders, bondholders, creditors, etc. On the other hand, common shares on average perform better than preferred shares or bonds over time.

a. Stock split
b. Growth investing
c. Common stock
d. 3M Company

49. The _____ is one of the basic financial statements as per Generally Accepted Accounting Principles, and it explains the changes in a company's retained earnings over the reporting period. It breaks down changes affecting the account, such as profits or losses from operations, dividends paid, and any other items charged or credited to retained earnings. A retained earnings statement is required by Generally Accepted Accounting Principles whenever comparative balance sheets and income statements are presented.

a. 3M Company
b. Notes to the financial statements
c. Financial statements
d. Statement of retained earnings

50. In corporate finance, _____ is a cash flow available for distribution among all the security holders of a company. They include equity holders, debt holders, preferred stock holders, convertible security holders, and so on.

a. Procurement
b. Tax profit
c. Product life cycle
d. Free cash flow

51. A _____ or stock divide increases or decreases the number of shares in a public company. The price is adjusted such that the before and after market capitalization of the company remains the same and dilution does not occur. Options and warrants are included.

a. Stockholder
b. Growth investing
c. 3M Company
d. Stock split

52. _____ is a financial ratio that indicates the percentage of a company's assets are provided via debt. It is the ratio of total debt (the sum of current liabilities and long-term liabilities) and total assets (the sum of current assets, fixed assets, and other assets such as 'goodwill'.)

$$\text{Debt ratio} = \frac{\text{Total Debt}}{\text{Total Assets}}$$

or alternatively:

$$\text{Debt ratio} = \frac{\text{Total Liability}}{\text{Total Assets}}$$

For example, a company with $2 million in total assets and $500,000 in total liabilities would have a _____ of 25%

Chapter 12. Reporting and Analyzing Cash Flows

Like all financial ratios, a company's _____ should be compared with their industry average or other competing firms.

a. Debt Ratio
c. 3M Company
b. Finance lease
d. Profitability index

53. In economics, business, retail, and accounting, a _____ is the value of money that has been used up to produce something, and hence is not available for use anymore. In economics, a _____ is an alternative that is given up as a result of a decision. In business, the _____ may be one of acquisition, in which case the amount of money expended to acquire it is counted as _____.

a. Cost
c. Cost of quality
b. Prime cost
d. Cost allocation

54. In financial accounting, _____ or cost of sales includes the direct costs attributable to the production of the goods sold by a company. This amount includes the materials cost used in creating the goods along with the direct labor costs used to produce the good. It excludes indirect expenses such as distribution costs and sales force costs.

a. FIFO and LIFO accounting
c. 3M Company
b. Reorder point
d. Cost of goods sold

55. _____ refers to a business or organization attempting to acquire goods or services to accomplish the goals of the enterprise. Though there are several organizations that attempt to set standards in the _____ process, processes can vary greatly between organizations. Typically the word e;_____e; is not used interchangeably with the word e;procuremente;, since procurement typically includes Expediting, Supplier Quality, and Traffic and Logistics (T'L) in addition to _____.

a. Free port
c. Consignor
b. Supply chain
d. Purchasing

Chapter 13. Analyzing and Interpreting Financial Statements

1. The general definition of an _____ is an evaluation of a person, organization, system, process, project or product. _____s are performed to ascertain the validity and reliability of information; also to provide an assessment of a system's internal control. The goal of an _____ is to express an opinion on the person/organization/system (etc) in question, under evaluation based on work done on a test basis.

   a. Audit
   b. Audit regime
   c. Assurance service
   d. Institute of Chartered Accountants of India

2. A _____ is a body of elected or appointed members who jointly oversee the activities of a company or organization. The body sometimes has a different name, such as board of trustees, board of governors, board of managers, or executive board. It is often simply referred to as 'the board.'

   A board's activities are determined by the powers, duties, and responsibilities delegated to it or conferred on it by an authority outside itself.

   a. Hospital Survey and Construction Act
   b. Consumer protection laws
   c. Chief Financial Officers Act of 1990
   d. Board of directors

3. A _____ is a party (e.g. person, organization, company, or government) that has a claim to the services of a second party. It is a person or institution to whom money is owed. The first party, in general, has provided some property or service to the second party under the assumption (usually enforced by contract) that the second party will return an equivalent property or service.

   a. Payback period
   b. Par value
   c. Creditor
   d. Treasury company

4. A _____, also client, buyer or purchaser is the buyer or user of the paid products of an individual or organization, mostly called the supplier or seller. This is typically through purchasing or renting goods or services.

   a. Customer
   b. BMC Software, Inc.
   c. 3M Company
   d. BNSF Railway

5. Employment is a contract between two parties, one being the employer and the other being the _____. An _____ may be defined as: 'A person in the service of another under any contract of hire, express or implied, oral or written, where the employer has the power or right to control and direct the _____ in the material details of how the work is to be performed.' Black's Law Dictionary page 471 (5th ed. 1979.)

   a. AIG
   b. AMEX
   c. ABC Television Network
   d. Employee

6. _____ of a business involves analyzing its financial statements and health, its management and competitive advantages, and its competitors and markets. The term is used to distinguish such analysis from other types of investment analysis, such as quantitative analysis and technical analysis.

   _____ is performed on historical and present data, but with the goal of making financial forecasts.

   a. 3M Company
   b. BNSF Railway
   c. BMC Software, Inc.
   d. Fundamental analysis

Chapter 13. Analyzing and Interpreting Financial Statements

7. A public utility (usually just utility) is an organization that maintains the infrastructure for a public service (often also providing a service using that infrastructure.) _____ are subject to forms of public control and regulation ranging from local community-based groups to state-wide government monopolies. Common arguments in favor of regulation include the desire to control market power, facilitate competition, promote investment or system expansion, or stabilize markets.
   a. BMC Software, Inc.
   b. 3M Company
   c. BNSF Railway
   d. Public utilities

8. A mutual shareholder or _____ is an individual or company (including a corporation) that legally owns one or more shares of stock in a joint stock company. A company's shareholders collectively own that company. Thus, the typical goal of such companies is to enhance shareholder value.
   a. Stock split
   b. Stockholder
   c. Growth investing
   d. 3M Company

9. _____ are formal records of a business' financial activities.

In British English, including United Kingdom company law, _____ are often referred to as accounts, although the term _____ is also used, particularly by accountants.

_____ provide an overview of a business' financial condition in both short and long term.

   a. Statement of retained earnings
   b. 3M Company
   c. Notes to the financial statements
   d. Financial statements

10. In finance, a _____ is a debt security, in which the authorized issuer owes the holders a debt and, depending on the terms of the _____, is obliged to pay interest (the coupon) and/or to repay the principal at a later date, termed maturity. It is a formal contract to repay borrowed money with interest at fixed intervals.

Thus a _____ is like a loan: the issuer is the borrower, the _____ holder is the lender, and the coupon is the interest.

   a. Coupon rate
   b. Zero-coupon bond
   c. Revenue bonds
   d. Bond

11. A _____ is a party that mediates between a buyer and a seller. A _____ who also acts as a seller or as a buyer becomes a principal party to the deal. Distinguish agent: one who acts on behalf of a principal.
   a. BNSF Railway
   b. BMC Software, Inc.
   c. Broker
   d. 3M Company

12. A _____ assesses the credit worthiness of an individual, corporation, or even a country. It is an evaluation made by credit bureaus of a borrower's overall credit history. They are calculated from financial history and current assets and liabilities.
   a. Debenture
   b. Debt
   c. Loan
   d. Credit rating

Chapter 13. Analyzing and Interpreting Financial Statements

13. A _____ is an annual report required by the U.S. Securities and Exchange Commission (SEC), that gives a comprehensive summary of a public company's performance. Although similarly named, the annual report on _____ is distinct from the often glossy 'annual report to shareholders', which a company must send to its shareholders when it holds an annual meeting to elect directors (though some companies combine the annual report and the 10-K into one document.) The 10-K includes information such as company history, organizational structure, executive compensation, equity, subsidiaries, and audited financial statements, among other information.

    a. Form 10-Q   b. Form 10-K
    c. 3M Company   d. Form 8-K

14. _____ is a business, economics or investment term that refers to an asset's ability to be easily converted through an act of buying or selling without causing a significant movement in the price and with minimum loss of value. Money, or cash on hand, is the most liquid asset. An act of exchange of a less liquid asset with a more liquid asset is called liquidation.

    a. Transfer agent   b. Spot rate
    c. Financial instruments   d. Market liquidity

15. A _____ is any one of a variety of different systems, institutions, procedures, social relations and infrastructures whereby persons trade, and goods and services are exchanged, forming part of the economy. It is an arrangement that allows buyers and sellers to exchange things. _____s vary in size, range, geographic scale, location, types and variety of human communities, as well as the types of goods and services traded.

    a. Market Failure   b. Perfect competition
    c. Recession   d. Market

16. In finance, or business _____ is the ability of an entity to pay its debts with available cash. _____ can also be described as the ability of a corporation to meet its long-term fixed expenses and to accomplish long-term expansion and growth. The better a company's _____, the better it is financially.

    a. Solvency   b. BMC Software, Inc.
    c. Capital asset   d. 3M Company

17. The basic _____ is the foundation for the double-entry bookkeeping system. It shows how assets were financed: either by borrowing money from someone (liability) or by paying your own money (shareholders' equity.)

        Assets = Liabilities + (Shareholders or Owners equity)

For example: A student buys a computer for $945.

    a. AMEX   b. AIG
    c. ABC Television Network   d. Accounting equation

18. A _____ is a computer application that simulates a paper worksheet. It displays multiple cells that together make up a grid consisting of rows and columns, each cell containing either alphanumeric text or numeric values. A _____ cell may alternatively contain a formula that defines how the contents of that cell is to be calculated from the contents of any other cell (or combination of cells) each time any cell is updated.

    a. Linear regression   b. Mutual fund
    c. Merck ' Co., Inc.   d. Spreadsheet

Chapter 13. Analyzing and Interpreting Financial Statements

19. _____ in economics and business is the result of an exchange and from that trade we assign a numerical monetary value to a good, service or asset. If Alice trades Bob 4 apples for an orange, the _____ of an orange is 4 apples. Inversely, the _____ of an apple is 1/4 oranges.

   a. Transactional Net Margin Method   b. Discounts and allowances

   c. Price discrimination   d. Price

20. In financial accounting, a _____ or statement of financial position is a summary of a person's or organization's balances. Assets, liabilities and ownership equity are listed as of a specific date, such as the end of its financial year. A _____ is often described as a snapshot of a company's financial condition.

   a. Balance sheet   b. 3M Company

   c. Statement of retained earnings   d. Financial statements

21. _____ is a company's financial statement that indicates how the revenue is transformed into the net income The purpose of the _____ is to show managers and investors whether the company made or lost money during the period being reported.

The important thing to remember about an _____ is that it represents a period of time.

   a. Income statement   b. AIG

   c. AMEX   d. ABC Television Network

22. The term '_____' refers to the concept of collecting information and attempting to spot a pattern in the information. In some fields of study, the term '_____' has more formally-defined meanings.

In project management _____ is a mathematical technique that uses historical results to predict future outcome.

   a. Regression analysis   b. 3M Company

   c. Multicollinearity   d. Trend analysis

23. In accounting, _____ has a very specific meaning. It is an outflow of cash or other valuable assets from a person or company to another person or company. This outflow of cash is generally one side of a trade for products or services that have equal or better current or future value to the buyer than to the seller.

   a. AMEX   b. AIG

   c. Expense   d. ABC Television Network

24. A _____ is the pinnacle activity involved in selling products or services in return for money or other compensation. It is an act of completion of a commercial activity.

A _____ is completed by the seller, the owner of the goods.

   a. Tertiary sector of economy   b. Maturity

   c. Sale   d. High yield stock

25. _____, in microeconomics, are the cost advantages that a business obtains due to expansion. They are factors that cause a producere;s average cost per unit to fall as scale is increased. _____ is a long run concept and refers to reductions in unit cost as the size of a facility, or scale, increases.

- a. Economies of scale
- b. AMEX
- c. ABC Television Network
- d. AIG

26. In economics, _____ or _____ goods or real _____ refers to factors of production used to create goods or services that are not themselves significantly consumed (though they may depreciate) in the production process. _____ goods may be acquired with money or financial _____. In finance and accounting, _____ generally refers to financial wealth, especially that used to start or maintain a business.

- a. Capital
- b. Vyborg Appeal
- c. Disclosure
- d. Screening

27. The _____ is a financial ratio that measures whether or not a firm has enough resources to pay its debts over the next 12 months. It compares a firm's current assets to its current liabilities. It is expressed as follows:

$$\text{Current ratio} = \frac{\text{Current Assets}}{\text{Current Liabilities}}$$

For example, if WXY Company's current assets are $50,000,000 and its current liabilities are $40,000,000, then its _____ would be $50,000,000 divided by $40,000,000, which equals 1.25.

- a. Net Interest Income
- b. Current ratio
- c. Return on capital
- d. Times interest earned

Chapter 13. Analyzing and Interpreting Financial Statements

28. _____ means the giving out of information, either voluntarily or to be in compliance with legal regulations or workplace rules.

- In Computer security, full _____ means disclosing full information about vulnerabilities.
- In computing, _____ widget
- Journalism, full _____ refers to disclosing the interests of the writer which may bear on the subject being written about, for example, if the writer has worked with an interview subject in the past.

- In law:
    - The law of England and Wales, _____ refers to a process that may form part of legal proceedings, whereby parties inform to other parties the existence of any relevant documents that are, or have been, in their control. This compares with the process known as discovery in the course of legal proceedings in the United States.
    - In U.S. civil procedure (litigation rules for civil cases), _____ is a stage prior to trial. In civil cases, each party must disclose to the opposing party the following: names of witnesses which it may use to support its side, copies of documents (or mere description of these documents) in its control which it may use to support its side, computation of damages claimed, and certain insurance information. _____ is related to, but technically prior to, the discovery stage.
    - In Company law (known as 'corporate law' in the United States), _____ refers to giving out information about public or limited companies or their officers, which might be kept secret if the company was a private company or a partnership.

- In real property transactions, _____ refers to providing to a buyer information known to the seller or broker/agent concerning the condition or other aspects of real property that would affect the property's value or desirability. These rules regarding what information must be disclosed, and whether the information must be disclosed even if a buyer does not ask, vary from one jurisdiction to the next.

    a. Disclosure
    b. Controlled Foreign Corporations
    c. Trailing
    d. Tax harmonisation

29. The _____ of 2002 (Pub.L. 107-204, 116 Stat. 745, enacted July 30, 2002), also known as the Public Company Accounting Reform and Investor Protection Act of 2002, is a United States federal law enacted on July 30, 2002 in response to a number of major corporate and accounting scandals including those affecting Enron, Tyco International, Adelphia, Peregrine Systems and WorldCom. The legislation establishes new or enhanced standards for all U.S. public company boards, management, and public accounting firms. It does not apply to privately held companies.
    a. Sarbanes-Oxley Act
    b. FCPA
    c. Fair Labor Standards Act
    d. Lease

30. _____ is a financial metric which represents operating liquidity available to a business. Along with fixed assets such as plant and equipment, _____ is considered a part of operating capital. It is calculated as current assets minus current liabilities.
    a. BMC Software, Inc.
    b. Working capital management
    c. Working capital
    d. 3M Company

Chapter 13. Analyzing and Interpreting Financial Statements

31. The _____, a ratio that is typically applied to banks, in simple terms is defined as expenses as a percentage of revenue (expenses / revenue), with a few variations. A lower percentage is better since that means expenses are low and earnings are high. It is related to operating leverage, which measures the ratio between fixed costs and variable costs.
   a. Operating leverage
   b. Average rate of return
   c. Efficiency ratio
   d. Equity ratio

32. In finance, the _____ or quick ratio or liquid ratio measures the ability of a company to use its near cash or quick assets to immediately extinguish or retire its current liabilities. Quick assets include those current assets that presumably can be quickly converted to cash at close to their book values.

$$\text{Quick (Acid Test) Ratio} = \frac{\text{Cash} + \text{Marketable Securities} + \text{Accounts Receivables}}{\text{Current Liabilities}}$$

Generally, the acid test ratio should be 1:1 or better, however this varies widely by industry.

   a. Invested capital
   b. Earnings per share
   c. Inventory turnover
   d. Acid-test

33. In business and accounting, _____ are everything of value that is owned by a person or company. It is a claim on the property your income of a borrower. The balance sheet of a firm records the monetary value of the _____ owned by the firm.
   a. Earnings before interest, taxes, depreciation and amortization
   b. Accounts receivable
   c. Accrual basis accounting
   d. Assets

34. In accounting, a _____ is an asset on the balance sheet which is expected to be sold or otherwise used up in the near future, usually within one year, or one business cycle - whichever is longer. Typical _____s include cash, cash equivalents, accounts receivable, inventory, the portion of prepaid accounts which will be used within a year, and short-term investments.

On the balance sheet, assets will typically be classified into _____s and long-term assets.

   a. General ledger
   b. Pro forma
   c. Deferred
   d. Current asset

35. _____ is a financial ratio that measures the efficiency of a company's use of its assets in generating sales revenue or sales income to the company.

$$\text{Asset Turnover} = \frac{Sales}{Average Total Assets}$$

- 'Sales' is the value of 'Net Sales' or 'Sales' from the company's income statement
- 'Average Total Assets' is the value of 'Total assets' from the company's balance sheet in the beginning and the end of the fiscal period divided by 2.

Chapter 13. Analyzing and Interpreting Financial Statements

a. Enterprise Value/Sales
c. Information ratio
b. Average propensity to consume
d. Asset turnover

36. In economics, the concept of the _____ refers to the decision-making time frame of a firm in which at least one factor of production is fixed. Costs which are fixed in the _____ have no impact on a firms decisions. For example a firm can raise output by increasing the amount of labour through overtime.
a. BMC Software, Inc.
b. Short-run
c. Long-run
d. 3M Company

37. The _____ is an equation that equals the cost of goods sold divided by the average inventory. Average inventory equals beginning inventory plus ending inventory divided by 2.

The formula for _____:

$$\text{Inventory Turnover} = \frac{\text{Cost of Goods Sold}}{\text{Average Inventory}}$$

The formula for average inventory:

$$\text{Average Inventory} = \frac{\text{Beginning inventory} + \text{Ending inventory}}{2}$$

A low turnover rate may point to overstocking, obsolescence, or deficiencies in the product line or marketing effort.

a. Inventory turnover
c. Earnings per share
b. Upside potential ratio
d. Enterprise Value/Sales

38. _____ is one of the Accounting Liquidity ratios, a financial ratio. This ratio measures the number of times, on average, the inventory is sold during the period. Its purpose is to measure the liquidity of the inventory.
a. Inventory turnover Ratio
b. Ending inventory
c. AIG
d. ABC Television Network

39. _____ is one of a series of accounting transactions dealing with the billing of customers who owe money to a person, company or organization for goods and services that have been provided to the customer. In most business entities this is typically done by generating an invoice and mailing or electronically delivering it to the customer, who in turn must pay it within an established timeframe called credit or payment terms.

An example of a common payment term is Net 30, meaning payment is due in the amount of the invoice 30 days from the date of invoice.

a. Accounts receivable
b. Accrual
c. Accrued revenue
d. Adjusting entries

Chapter 13. Analyzing and Interpreting Financial Statements

40. _____ is one of the accounting liquidity ratios, a financial ratio. This ratio measures the number of times, on average, receivables (e.g. Accounts Receivable) are collected during the period. A popular variant of the _____ is to convert it into an Average Collection Period in terms of days.
   a. Price-to-sales ratio
   b. Receivable turnover Ratio
   c. Capital
   d. Shrinkage

41. In finance, _____ refers to the way a corporation finances its assets through some combination of equity, debt, or hybrid securities. A firm's _____ is then the composition or 'structure' of its liabilities. For example, a firm that sells $20 billion in equity and $80 billion in debt is said to be 20% equity-financed and 80% debt-financed.
   a. Capital structure
   b. Restricted stock
   c. Gross income
   d. Flow-through entity

42. _____ is that which is owed; usually referencing assets owed, but the term can also cover moral obligations and other interactions not requiring money. In the case of assets, _____ is a means of using future purchasing power in the present before a summation has been earned. Some companies and corporations use _____ as a part of their overall corporate finance strategy.
   a. Loan
   b. Lender
   c. Debenture
   d. Debt

43. _____ is a financial ratio that indicates the percentage of a company's assets are provided via debt. It is the ratio of total debt (the sum of current liabilities and long-term liabilities) and total assets (the sum of current assets, fixed assets, and other assets such as 'goodwill'.)

$$\text{Debt ratio} = \frac{\text{Total Debt}}{\text{Total Assets}}$$

or alternatively:

$$\text{Debt ratio} = \frac{\text{Total Liability}}{\text{Total Assets}}$$

For example, a company with $2 million in total assets and $500,000 in total liabilities would have a _____ of 25%

Like all financial ratios, a company's _____ should be compared with their industry average or other competing firms.

   a. Profitability index
   b. 3M Company
   c. Finance lease
   d. Debt ratio

44. The _____ is a financial ratio indicating the relative proportion of equity to all used to finance a company's assets. The two components are often taken from the firm's balance sheet or statement of financial position (so-called book value), but the ratio may also be calculated using market values for both, if the company's equities are publicly traded.

Chapter 13. Analyzing and Interpreting Financial Statements

The _____ is especially in Central Europe a very common financial ratio while in the US the debt to _____ is more often used in financial (research) reports.

a. Average accounting return
c. Earnings yield
b. Efficiency ratio
d. Equity ratio

45. _____ in business is an accounting concept that refers to ownership of a company (subsidiary) that is less than 50% of outstanding shares. _____ belongs to other investors and is reported on the consolidated balance sheet of the owning company to reflect the claim on assets belonging to other, non-controlling shareholders. Also, _____ is reported on the consolidated income statement as a share of profit belonging to minority shareholders.

a. Bankruptcy prediction
c. Minority interest
b. Subledger
d. Credit memo

46. _____ is a fee paid on borrowed assets. It is the price paid for the use of borrowed money, or, money earned by deposited funds .Assets that are sometimes lent with _____ include money, shares, consumer goods through hire purchase, major assets such as aircraft, and even entire factories in finance lease arrangements. The _____ is calculated upon the value of the assets in the same manner as upon money.

a. AIG
c. Interest
b. ABC Television Network
d. Insolvency

47. In financial accounting, a _____ is defined as an obligation of an entity arising from past transactions or events, the settlement of which may result in the transfer or use of assets, provision of services or other yielding of economic benefits in the future.

a. Vested
c. False Claims Act
b. Liability
d. Corporate governance

48. _____ or interest coverage ratio is a measure of a company's ability to honor its debt payments. It may be calculated as either EBIT or EBITDA divided by the total interest payable.

a. Times interest earned
c. Yield Gap
b. Capital recovery factor
d. Return of capital

49. _____, net margin, net _____ or net profit ratio all refer to a measure of profitability. It is calculated by finding the net profit as a percentage of the revenue.

$$\text{Net profit margin} = \frac{\text{Net profit (after taxes)}}{\text{Revenue}} \times 100$$

The _____ is mostly used for internal comparison.

Chapter 13. Analyzing and Interpreting Financial Statements

a. 3M Company
b. BNSF Railway
c. BMC Software, Inc.
d. Profit margin

50. _____ is an equity (stock) exchange located at 11 Wall Street in lower Manhattan, New York, USA.) It is the largest stock exchange in the world by dollar value of its listed companies' securities. As of October 2008, the combined capitalization of all domestic _____ listed companies was US$10.1 trillion.

a. New York Stock Exchange
b. BNSF Railway
c. 3M Company
d. BMC Software, Inc.

51. A _____, (formerly a securities exchange) is a corporation or mutual organization which provides 'trading' facilities for stock brokers and traders, to trade stocks and other securities. _____s also provide facilities for the issue and redemption of securities as well as other financial instruments and capital events including the payment of income and dividends. The securities traded on a _____ include: shares issued by companies, unit trusts, derivatives, pooled investment products and bonds.

a. BMC Software, Inc.
b. 3M Company
c. BNSF Railway
d. Stock Exchange

52. _____ are payments made by a corporation to its shareholder members. It is the portion of corporate profits paid out to stockholders. When a corporation earns a profit or surplus, that money can be put to two uses: it can either be re-invested in the business (called retained earnings), or it can be paid to the shareholders as a dividend.

a. Dividends
b. Dividend payout ratio
c. Dividend stripping
d. Dividend yield

53. The _____ on a company stock is the company's annual dividend payments divided by its market cap, or the dividend per share divided by the price per share. It is often expressed as a percentage.

Dividend payments on preferred shares are stipulated by the prospectus.

a. Dividends
b. Dividend payout ratio
c. Dividend stripping
d. Dividend yield

54. _____ is typically a 'higher ranking' stock than voting shares, and its terms are negotiated between the corporation and the investor.

_____ usually carries no voting rights, but may carry superior priority over common stock in the payment of dividends and upon liquidation. _____ may carry a dividend that is paid out prior to any dividends being paid to common stock holders.

a. Preferred stock
b. Cash flow
c. Restricted stock
d. Gross income

55. In finance, the term _____ describes the amount in cash that returns to the owners of a security. Normally it does not include the price variations, at the difference of the total return. _____ applies to various stated rates of return on stocks (common and preferred, and convertible), fixed income instruments (bonds, notes, bills, strips, zero coupon), and some other investment type insurance products (e.g. annuities).

Chapter 13. Analyzing and Interpreting Financial Statements

a. Pension System
c. Disclosure
b. Residence trusts
d. Yield

56. In accounting, _____ or carrying value is the value of an asset according to its balance sheet account balance. For assets, the value is based on the original cost of the asset less any depreciation, amortization or impairment costs made against the asset. Traditionally, a company's _____ is its total assets minus intangible assets and liabilities.

a. Matching principle
c. Depreciation
b. Generally accepted accounting principles
d. Book value

57. _____ is a form of corporation equity ownership represented in the securities. It is a stock whose dividends are based on market fluctuations. It is dangerous in comparison to preferred shares and some other investment options, in that in the event of bankruptcy, _____ investors receive their funds after preferred stock holders, bondholders, creditors, etc. On the other hand, common shares on average perform better than preferred shares or bonds over time.

a. Growth investing
c. 3M Company
b. Stock split
d. Common stock

58. _____ is a specific term used in companies' financial reporting from the company-whole point of view. Because that use excludes the effects of changing ownership interest, an economic measure of _____ is necessary for financial analysis from the shareholders' point of view

_____ is defined by the Financial Accounting Standards Board, or FASB, as 'the change in equity [net assets] of a business enterprise during a period from transactions and other events and circumstances from nonowner sources. It includes all changes in equity during a period except those resulting from investments by owners and distributions to owners.'

_____ is the sum of net income and other items that must bypass the income statement because they have not been realized, including items like an unrealized holding gain or loss from available for sale securities and foreign currency translation gains or losses.

a. Comprehensive income
c. 3M Company
b. BNSF Railway
d. BMC Software, Inc.

59. _____ are the earnings returned on the initial investment amount.

In the US, the Financial Accounting Standards Board (FASB) requires companies' income statements to report _____ for each of the major categories of the income statement: continuing operations, discontinued operations, extraordinary items, and net income.

The _____ formula does not include preferred dividends for categories outside of continued operations and net income.

a. Earnings yield
c. Invested capital
b. Average accounting return
d. Earnings per share

60. _____, Gross profit margin or Gross Profit Rate can be defined as the amount of contribution to the business enterprise, after paying for direct-fixed and direct-variable unit costs, required to cover overheads (fixed commitments) and provide a buffer for unknown items. It expresses the relationship between gross profit and sales revenue.

It can be expressed in absolute terms:

Gross Profit = Revenue − Cost of Goods Sold

or as the ratio of gross profit to sales revenue, usually in the form of a percentage:

_____ Percentage = (Revenue-Cost of Goods Sold)/Revenue

Cost of goods sold includes variable costs and fixed costs directly linked to the product, such as material and labor.

   a. BMC Software, Inc.
   c. BNSF Railway
   b. Gross margin
   d. 3M Company

61. An _____ is a period with reference to which United Kingdom corporation tax is charged. It helps dictate when tax is paid on income and gains. An _____ begins whenever a company comes within the corporation tax charge, and whenever an _____ ends without the company ceasing to be within the charge.
   a. AIG
   c. Accounting period
   b. ABC Television Network
   d. AMEX

62. _____ is a term used with respect to a retailed product, indicating that the product is in the end of its product lifetime and a vendor will no longer be marketing, selling, or promoting a particular product and may also be limiting or ending support for the product. In the specific case of product sales, the term end-of-sale (EOS) has also been used. The term lifetime, after the last production date, depends on the product and is related to a customer's expected product lifetime.
   a. AMEX
   c. ABC Television Network
   b. End-of-life
   d. AIG

63. _____ is the term used to refer to the standard framework of guidelines for financial accounting used in any given jurisdiction. _____ includes the standards, conventions, and rules accountants follow in recording and summarizing transactions, and in the preparation of financial statements.

Financial accounting information must be assembled and reported objectively.

   a. Long-term liabilities
   c. General ledger
   b. Current asset
   d. Generally accepted accounting principles

64. A _____ proof is a mathematical proof that a particular theory is consistent. The early development of mathematical proof theory was driven by the desire to provide finitary _____ proofs for all of mathematics as part of Hilbert's program. Hilbert's program was strongly impacted by incompleteness theorems, which showed that sufficiently strong proof theories cannot prove their own _____

Chapter 13. Analyzing and Interpreting Financial Statements

a. Consistency
b. Monte Carlo methods
c. Daybook
d. Consumption

65. _____ is a subsection in equity where 'other comprehensive income' is accumulated (summed or 'aggregated'.)

The balance of _____ is presented in the Equity section of the Balance Sheet as is the Retained Earnings balance, which aggregates past and current Earnings, and past and current Dividends.

Other comprehensive income is the difference between net income and comprehensive income and represents the certain gains and losses of the enterprise.

a. Authorised capital
b. Accumulated other comprehensive income
c. Inventory turnover ratio
d. Operating budget

ANSWER KEY

Chapter 1
1. d	2. a	3. c	4. d	5. c	6. c	7. d	8. d	9. d	10. b
11. a	12. c	13. a	14. a	15. d	16. d	17. d	18. d	19. c	20. c
21. d	22. d	23. c	24. c	25. d	26. b	27. d	28. d	29. d	30. b
31. d	32. b	33. b	34. d	35. d	36. c	37. d	38. d	39. a	40. d
41. d	42. d	43. b	44. b	45. a	46. a	47. d	48. d	49. c	50. b
51. d	52. b	53. d	54. a	55. c	56. d	57. b	58. b	59. a	60. b
61. a	62. d	63. c	64. d	65. a	66. b	67. c	68. d	69. a	70. d
71. b	72. d	73. d	74. d	75. d	76. d	77. d	78. d	79. d	

Chapter 2
1. d	2. c	3. d	4. b	5. c	6. a	7. a	8. b	9. c	10. d
11. d	12. a	13. c	14. b	15. d	16. d	17. d	18. d	19. d	20. a
21. c	22. b	23. c	24. d	25. c	26. d	27. b	28. b	29. d	30. d
31. d	32. d	33. b	34. d	35. a	36. b	37. d	38. d	39. d	40. b
41. d	42. a	43. d	44. d	45. d	46. d	47. c	48. d	49. d	50. b
51. d	52. b	53. c	54. d						

Chapter 3
1. d	2. c	3. d	4. d	5. d	6. c	7. d	8. d	9. a	10. d
11. b	12. d	13. a	14. d	15. d	16. d	17. c	18. d	19. b	20. c
21. d	22. d	23. d	24. d	25. d	26. a	27. d	28. d	29. b	30. d
31. a	32. a	33. c	34. b	35. c	36. d	37. d	38. d	39. d	40. d
41. a	42. d	43. d	44. b	45. a	46. b	47. b	48. c	49. d	50. b
51. b	52. a	53. d	54. b	55. d	56. b	57. c	58. a	59. d	60. b
61. d	62. b	63. d							

Chapter 4
1. a	2. d	3. a	4. d	5. a	6. d	7. a	8. d	9. c	10. c
11. d	12. d	13. c	14. a	15. a	16. a	17. b	18. c	19. b	20. d
21. c	22. b	23. b	24. b	25. b	26. d	27. a	28. c	29. d	30. b
31. d	32. d	33. d	34. a	35. d	36. a	37. c	38. b	39. d	

Chapter 5
1. a	2. c	3. d	4. a	5. b	6. d	7. b	8. d	9. c	10. a
11. a	12. d	13. d	14. b	15. d	16. c	17. d	18. b	19. b	20. b
21. a	22. d	23. c	24. d	25. d	26. d	27. d	28. d	29. d	30. d
31. c	32. c								

ANSWER KEY

Chapter 6

1. d	2. d	3. d	4. b	5. b	6. d	7. b	8. a	9. a	10. c
11. d	12. a	13. c	14. d	15. d	16. d	17. b	18. b	19. d	20. d
21. b	22. c	23. a	24. b	25. d	26. b	27. b	28. c	29. c	30. c
31. a	32. d	33. d	34. d	35. c	36. b	37. d	38. d	39. d	40. d
41. c	42. c	43. c	44. c	45. d	46. c	47. d	48. b	49. a	50. a
51. b	52. c	53. d	54. d	55. b	56. c	57. d	58. d	59. d	60. d
61. d	62. d	63. d	64. c	65. d					

Chapter 7

1. b	2. a	3. d	4. d	5. b	6. d	7. a	8. d	9. d	10. c
11. d	12. d	13. b	14. c	15. c	16. d	17. c	18. b	19. c	20. d
21. b	22. d	23. d	24. b	25. c	26. b	27. d	28. d	29. c	30. d
31. d	32. b	33. d	34. c	35. d	36. a	37. a			

Chapter 8

1. d	2. d	3. b	4. d	5. a	6. b	7. c	8. d	9. d	10. b
11. d	12. d	13. b	14. a	15. d	16. d	17. d	18. d	19. d	20. d
21. d	22. d	23. b	24. d	25. d	26. c	27. a	28. a	29. d	30. b
31. b	32. a	33. d	34. d	35. b	36. a	37. d	38. a	39. d	40. b
41. b	42. d	43. c	44. c	45. d	46. c	47. d	48. b	49. d	50. a
51. b	52. b	53. b	54. d						

Chapter 9

1. d	2. d	3. d	4. d	5. d	6. c	7. a	8. d	9. a	10. d
11. b	12. a	13. a	14. c	15. d	16. d	17. d	18. c	19. d	20. d
21. d	22. a	23. a	24. b	25. d	26. d	27. d	28. d	29. b	30. d
31. d	32. b	33. d	34. d	35. d	36. c	37. d	38. a	39. d	40. c
41. c	42. c	43. d	44. d	45. a	46. b	47. a	48. d	49. d	50. c
51. c	52. c	53. c	54. d	55. c	56. c	57. d	58. d	59. a	60. d

Chapter 10

1. c	2. d	3. d	4. c	5. d	6. d	7. d	8. b	9. d	10. a
11. a	12. d	13. c	14. d	15. d	16. d	17. d	18. d	19. d	20. d
21. b	22. c	23. d	24. c	25. d	26. b	27. d	28. d	29. d	30. d
31. a	32. d	33. d	34. d	35. b	36. c	37. d	38. a	39. b	40. a
41. a	42. d	43. c	44. d	45. d	46. c	47. d	48. d	49. c	50. d
51. d	52. a	53. b	54. a	55. b	56. d	57. d	58. b	59. d	60. b
61. c	62. d								

Chapter 11

1. b	2. b	3. a	4. a	5. a	6. b	7. d	8. d	9. d	10. a
11. d	12. d	13. c	14. d	15. a	16. d	17. a	18. a	19. d	20. b
21. d	22. a	23. d	24. a	25. a	26. d	27. d	28. d	29. d	30. c
31. d	32. c	33. d	34. a	35. d	36. a	37. d	38. a	39. d	40. d
41. c	42. b	43. a	44. a	45. d	46. a	47. a	48. d	49. a	50. d
51. d	52. a	53. d	54. b	55. c	56. a	57. d	58. d	59. a	60. d
61. c	62. c	63. d							

Chapter 12

1. b	2. d	3. d	4. a	5. d	6. b	7. c	8. c	9. a	10. d
11. b	12. d	13. d	14. d	15. c	16. a	17. a	18. b	19. a	20. d
21. d	22. d	23. d	24. c	25. d	26. c	27. d	28. a	29. d	30. b
31. d	32. d	33. d	34. a	35. d	36. d	37. b	38. b	39. b	40. c
41. d	42. c	43. a	44. b	45. a	46. d	47. d	48. c	49. d	50. d
51. d	52. a	53. a	54. d	55. d					

Chapter 13

1. a	2. d	3. c	4. a	5. d	6. d	7. d	8. b	9. d	10. d
11. c	12. d	13. b	14. d	15. d	16. a	17. d	18. d	19. d	20. a
21. a	22. d	23. c	24. c	25. a	26. a	27. b	28. a	29. a	30. c
31. c	32. d	33. d	34. d	35. d	36. b	37. a	38. a	39. a	40. b
41. a	42. d	43. d	44. d	45. c	46. c	47. b	48. a	49. d	50. a
51. d	52. a	53. d	54. a	55. d	56. d	57. d	58. a	59. d	60. b
61. c	62. b	63. d	64. a	65. b					

www.ingramcontent.com/pod-product-compliance
Lightning Source LLC
Chambersburg PA
CBHW082205230426
43672CB00015B/2913